D0044543

TAKE YOU WHEREVER YOU GO

TAKE YOU WHEREVER YOU GO

KENNY LEON
with John Hassan

FOREWORD BY SAMUEL L. JACKSON

GRAND CENTRAL
PUBLISHING

NEW YORK   BOSTON

Grand Central Publishing
Hachette Book Group
1290 Avenue of the Americas, New York, NY 10104
grandcentralpublishing.com
twitter.com/grandcentralpub

First edition: June 2018

Grand Central Publishing is a division of Hachette Book Group, Inc. The Grand Central Publishing name and logo is a trademark of Hachette Book Group, Inc.

The publisher is not responsible for websites (or their content) that are not owned by the publisher.

Library of Congress Cataloging-in-Publication Data has been applied for.

ISBNs: 978-1-5387-4497-0 (hardcover), 978-1-5387-4496-3 (ebook)

Printed in the United States of America

LSC-C

10 9 8 7 6 5 4 3 2 1

To Grandma Mamie, who helped me understand that crying and laughing are both good things.
To Annie Ruth, who taught me that anything is possible.
To August Wilson, who showed me the beauty of being a committed artist.
To my two-year-old grandson Gabriel Nuytemans, in hope that his world is safe and beautiful.
To the children of today—may they understand that success doesn't belong to a neighborhood or a chosen family but to the many who have a vision and put in the work.

Contents

Foreword

There is a term that has popped up lately for people who make the world a better place—"agents for change," which fits Kenny Leon perfectly. The theater communities he's touched while on his journey are all reflections of his vision of inclusion and diversity. It's humbling to know I was part of what set him on his path when he saw a play at Spelman College that lit his artistic fire. There were many of us treading the boards, sharing dreams, meals, joy, and a dedication to an impossible dream that our backgrounds and parental expectations never offered us. I'm not sure when Kenny decided he was more interested in directing than acting, but when it happened, the theater scene in Atlanta was altered permanently. I do know that by the time he left the Alliance Theatre, he had altered the audience demographic, and the plays presented reflected the diversity of the Atlanta community. His choices and outreach educated the old guard audience and inspired an excluded and younger audience to come to a place that had been culturally and literally closed to them. The True Colors Theatre Company, which he started, continues to be the cultural melting pot he envisioned. His Broadway ventures have been audience broadening also, enticing younger audiences through innovative casting and the subject matter of the plays. Accepting the challenge of "live televised plays," I saw a twinkle in his eyes that let me know just how excited he was to pull in this new audience and explore a new medium. His success was no surprise. Winning the Tony, the Emmy nomination, the recognitions of achievement that are coming now, are all by-products of Kenny's dedication to art as a tool for change. It's been a joy to watch and at times be an active participant in Kenny's gift to the world.

—*Samuel L. Jackson*

I.

Grandma Mamie

My life is the answer to generational prayers.

Mamie Wilson was my grandmother. Her words are the words I live by.

I went to live with her when I was four years old and stayed about four years. She'd already raised thirteen kids of her own when I showed up. And she'd already lived a very hard life.

"Mamie" isn't short for something. It's a good Southern name. It suited her, too. Simple, direct, endearing.

Grandma Mamie was about five feet six and noticeably bow-legged. And very strong. She had hazel-brown eyes, high cheekbones, and a Native American cast to her features. Her skin tone was beautiful, like coffee with cream. Her strong hands were more of a caramel color. She didn't have calluses, but her veins popped along the backs of her hands. She pulled back her grayish-silver hair so that the contours of her roundish head were visible. She was big-boned but not particularly heavy or fat. She never went around screaming or hollering at anybody. Her voice was strong but even-keeled. She liked to laugh and told her stories with enthusiasm and humor.

Mamie Roberts was born in 1905 in Tallahassee, Florida. She married twenty-five-year-old Perman Wilson in 1925 and was pregnant nearly every year until 1944. She had thirteen children and four miscarriages. Simply put, she was in a marriage in which that was what you did. The farm wasn't going to farm itself. And they couldn't afford to hire the work out.

And to be honest, she was alone in that marriage. My grandfather's main contribution to the family was, well, to make the family. He was happy to help produce the children needed to work their farm. But he wasn't attentive to home life or the raising of the family.

When I was much older, my grandma often sat me down on the porch and shared more mature and intimate details about her life. *My husband used to mess around with my cousin.* He treated my grandma very poorly. I heard other things, too, but that's the story.

My mother, Annie Ruth Wilson, loved her father but also saw him clearly. No bitterness was ever passed along to me. That's just the way he was. He died before I was born so I have only their words to go on, but they've yet to steer me wrong. The truth is powerful and you should always face it.

I can hear Grandma Mamie now.

Baby, it was rough. It was rough. I had to pull the plow.

My grandmother lived hard but without complaint. She bore those children, cleaned, cooked, and plowed the fields like an animal. I say that with love, awe, and respect. She strapped on the yoke and *pulled the plow.* Instead of a mule. That image has stayed with me.

"Oh, *you* out there pulling the plow!"

Every time I have a tough day at work or just get frustrated by everyday concerns, I think of my grandmother's life in those days. It's a perspective that I keep close by, and it has helped me all my life.

That farm work was backbreaking but it was all there was. Working the farm. Mamie got up and fixed breakfast and then went out and worked the fields. Then she fixed lunch and went back out to the fields. Then she fixed dinner. After a full day in the fields, she came home and fed those kids, did laundry, folded clothes, helped with homework, and gave all those good night kisses and hugs.

My grandma Mamie put in those endless days of work and effort and her kids never missed a meal. She led that life, that hard, country life, without the comfort of a partnership and some love coming back.

During all of this time, and all of her life really, there was prayer. A strong belief in God. Prayers of every kind: for happiness, health, and good weather; for her children's well-being and safety; for a better life to come. For all who will come in the years ahead.

I pray I'm the last one in this family to pull a plow.
Can you see to that for me, Lord?
I hope the world will be a lot better for Kenny as he grows up.
I hope he can shape his life into what he wants it to be.

* * *

Grandma Mamie prayed me into existence. She prayed that her children, and their children, would have better lives than she did.

She knew in her bones that life could be better than the way she lived in those twenty-five years on that farm.

She knew little about my line of work. Acting, directing, the theater. She certainly knew about movies and plays and such. But it would never have occurred to her that you could make a living in that world. In her world, the job possibilities were narrow and predictable. Farmer. Domestic. Teacher. Preacher. Factory worker. Waitress. Cook. Doctor. Lawyer. Familiar and important jobs that made the world go 'round.

But her steady support led me to believe I could go for my dreams, once I figured them out. She wanted a better life for me than the one she had, and she wanted me to define what "better" meant. She wanted me to have choices. Possibilities. Freedom. She wanted my life to come from my ideas about life.

So many times on her porch she'd look at me and say, *Oh, you always gotta laugh. You gotta laugh, baby. You always gotta laugh! Find stuff to laugh at!*

She was giving me a jewel for my life.

You gotta laugh! If you keep laughin', and if you're not afraid to cry, you will be better in this world. You will discover your passion and you will be better. You gotta find the laughter.

Her love and encouragement were the fuel for my dreams, for my willingness to dream. She made sure I knew that I could do whatever I set my mind to do. That's a powerful gift to give a young soul, that belief in self. That belief in belonging. That belief in opportunities. And I always look for the laughter.

This book is my continuation of her prayers. This book is my way of telling you, as she told me, that you can do whatever you want to do. The only limits are the ones you set yourself. You have all you need in you right now.

She carried me then. I carry her today.

Annie Ruth

I don't have a lot of use for Father's Day. For me, it's a trumped-up, forced celebration and I ignore it. But I never miss Mother's Day or my mother's birthday.

My mother was born Annie Ruth Wilson in Tallahassee, Florida, in 1940, the tenth of thirteen children born to Mamie and Perman Wilson. They had seven sons and six daughters.

She is about five feet six inches tall with charcoal black skin tone, darker than her mother's, and the most beautiful skin complexion in the world. She always had beautiful skin, soft and smooth to the touch. She used Jergens lotion every day, and I figured that was the key. So I started using it myself, and that distinct aroma will always remind me of my mother.

In her youth, she had long, silky, flowing black hair that was a little darker than her skin. As she aged, she cut her hair into a closely cropped, short, gray Afro. I don't know if that is how she would describe it, but that works for me. And I love how she looks. She'll occasionally wear wigs, and the short hair makes that easier.

My mother is conservative in many ways. She is a real, true, honest Christian. She believes in and lives by the values of her faith. God is first in her life. And my mother believes in faith, hope, love, justice, and service to others. She has a quiet but forceful dignity in her religious approach to this life, and it very much defines her.

My mother grew into her Christian life. She gave birth to me while unmarried and at the age of fifteen. When I was a young boy, I remember her dancing the Camel Walk and singing along to James Brown. But she grew past that and was a much different woman at twenty-five than she was at fifteen.

She wears very simple dresses that go below the knee. On Sunday, she dresses up and her jewelry will be a simple necklace with short earbobs. She might wear an usher's uniform, too, depending on what she has to do each week. But no matter what she is wearing or what she has to do, she will carry her simple, natural beauty.

Also unlike her bolder and more demonstrative mother, my mother enters a room softly. Not sneakily, just softly. She just appears.

Oh, she's here.

I can't remember ever waking up before my mother. Whenever I woke up, I would hear her moving and talking quietly down the short hallway of our home.

Oh, she's there.

For as long as I can remember, my mother had a quiet sense of truth about her. She wasn't full of herself, but she was always confident and sure.

It might have come from my experience of living alone with my grandmother, but around the time I was eight or nine, I developed a bond with my mother based on talking with her. I'd had my grandmother's undivided attention and had grown used to it. My mother and I developed a habit of having very intimate, serious conversations around the sink, whether she was cooking or I was doing dishes. We have always been able to communicate openly and honestly. We are used to confiding in each other. I think that Grandma and Mom both instilled that in me, an appreciation for conversation and a willingness to be present for other people. I learned from them how important trust is. And trust is at the heart of everything I do as a director.

When I was growing up, I remember always being able to go to my mom with questions I had, about anything, or conflicts I had about something in the Bible.

One time I asked her, "Can you get to Heaven if you just treat everybody nice and respectful?"

"Oh, no, Kenny, you need to do certain things," she said. "Read a bit more of the Bible."

Later, I said, "Yes, Mama, I think if you treat people nicely and respectfully, that's really all you need to get to Heaven."

"Well, if you can work that out between you and the Lord, that's good."

I've always liked that answer. The open-ended nature of it allowed me to learn how to find my own answers. She certainly didn't agree with me, but she kept that to herself. She was encouraging me to think for myself, leading me to learn how to come to my own conclusions.

Her approach made her easy to talk to, about any subject. Growing up, if I had a conflict, a struggle, or a tough decision to weigh, she was the one I would call. I still do. That's a rare bond between generations and I'm grateful.

She never varied. She told me what she felt and then left time and room for me to find my own answers. She never told me what to think or do. And she never chastised me for landing on a different position from hers.

One time, I was studying the Bible and told her that I saw a conflict between the fire and brimstone and wrath of God and killing in the Old Testament and the relatively peaceful life of Jesus in the New Testament.

She saw no contradiction. She said it was all truthful and honest and that those two books made up the Holy Scriptures. Her knowledge of the Bible is impressive, and she could quote me chapter and verse to illustrate her points. I usually went back and thought about it some more and sometimes I ended up even more confused. But I developed a habit of checking in with her spiritually.

Whenever I get stuck in life, I ask my mom if the Bible has insight on whatever I'm facing.

When I was struggling with money in college, I asked my mom, "What does God have to say about finances?"

And she'd say that you have to read Matthew, chapter 6, verse 4. Or Paul's letter to Timothy.

She always had a good, helpful answer.

She was also ready to handle any response I might have if I thought there were inconsistencies in the Bible. Or contradictions, like the differences I'd observed between the Old Testament God and New Testament Jesus. "Mom, it says here…"

"But you don't know who's saying that!"

"What do you mean?"

"Saul was writing this as a letter from so-and-so, and that was in 15-something B.C. Or that was before God destroyed the world the first time." Or whatever her specific response would be.

"Oh. I didn't know that. I'm just taking it out of context."

"You can't take things out of context. You have to know who said it, when they said it, to whom they were talking, and why they said it."

When I got older, she raised the stakes a little bit. She would say, "I want you to defend what you're saying. But don't use what I believe to defend what you're saying. Try that."

I'd start in with what she had just said and she'd stop me.

"No, no, no. Tell me what you believe. But your belief can't be just saying, 'I don't believe what you believe.'"

She instilled in me the value of being able to back up your opinions or your interpretations of a text. And she instructed me to search for myself, to live for myself.

What do you know?

What do you not know?

What do you believe?

Can you explain your belief with more than just a dismissing of someone else's beliefs?

When it came to matters of spirituality and faith, she was just as rigorous.

What do you choose to believe?

Why?

My mother never told me how to answer any of these questions. But she certainly encouraged me to ask them. This raising, or training, is part of me now. I don't do things superficially, certainly not important things.

As an adult, I continued to use my mom as a touchstone and a resource. I valued her opinion and perspective because she had given me so much room to find my own. From Atlanta or New York, I would, and still do, call her when considering a play to direct.

In 1994, I was the artistic director of the Alliance Theatre in Atlanta. I was contemplating staging Tony Kushner's *Angels in America: Millennium Approaches*. After its initial Broadway run, the play was released to four theaters and ours was one of them.

I thought it was a tremendous play, and I regard Kushner as an amazing writer. I have always respected him. And he was giving me an opportunity to take on this masterpiece.

I called my mother.

"I have a chance to put on this amazing play," I said. "But I don't know how it will play in the South. Mom, in this play, gay male characters are kissing each other. There's nudity. And the subject matter explored is very mature and a little controversial."

At that time, I was in my first season as artistic director at the Alliance. I was becoming a successful, semifamous director. My mother and my stepfather were proud of everything I was doing and tried to see everything I was working on.

We discussed it a bit more and then she said, "You have to do that play, Kenny. That play is an important play. I know you'll do a wonderful job with it.

"But you know, I can't see it."

Again, I loved that answer. I respected her so much for that. *Angels in America* was something she could not see, but that didn't make it something I could not do.

That answer fits in with the way she always talked to me. She's very consistent and very straightforward, and again, she left me the room to make my own decision.

I think part of our closeness and ability to talk about things so easily is that she is only fifteen years older than I am. We can relate to each other a little easier than parents and children with more years between them.

I have many fond memories of being around my mother and always trying to talk to her. It didn't matter if there were other people around. When I go home, one of the things I most enjoy is finding my mom in her kitchen and pulling up a stool or a chair and talking with her.

"How you doin', Ma? How you really doin'?"

She'll ask me about what play I might do. And I'll catch up on how everything is going at church. And I hope that never ends.

Sometimes I will pray and ask God about my mother and me.

Lord, have I been the kind of son my mother wanted me to be?

Am I living the way she wanted me to?

Am I doing right by her?

Does she know how much I love her?

Please make sure she knows.

A few years ago my mother sent me a card in which she told me what kind of son I have been to her:

"My life could not be what it is without your contributions to it. I would never have seen a play on Broadway. I would never have met Phylicia Rashad. I wouldn't have traveled to Hawaii. I am grateful for our relationship and how you have taken care of me and stayed close."

That's not the kind of card you get when you're young, if at all. But for her to take the time to articulate that was very meaningful to me.

My mother had found yet another way to answer my prayers.

Living with Mamie

I was born on February 10, 1956. My parents never married so my mother lived with her mother for a time after I was born. Then she lived on her own in an apartment. She and my father continued to see each other and their family grew.

By 1960, my mother was nineteen with two children, my sister Jackie having joined the family in 1958. And she was pregnant with my brother Tony. She was feeling a bit trapped and needed to make a change from her life in Tallahassee with my father. She felt that life was holding her back from reaching her potential. My father, Leroy Leon, who was about to have his third child with my mother, didn't agree but my mother took some brave steps. They were not bound legally to each other, so despite their close relationship, my mother retained a sense of independence.

My mother always had aspirations but had not done much about them. Eventually, however, she realized that if she was going to have any hope of making her life like the one she dreamed of, she was going to have to move away. Her dreams were not specific. The main idea was change. A fresh start.

If she stayed, her life would inevitably have been just more of the same. She would be the mother of more children, and she would still be around her family and still be around the farm. She'd remain the barefoot country girl she'd always been. She'd lived that life for almost twenty years and wanted more. My mother had also seen her parents' marriage clearly. She loved her dad but she also knew the truth. She knew her father was a ladies' man and wasn't always around. She knew that her mother was the stronger one, the provider, and that her mother was unhappy. She saw all of that.

She took my sister and moved 300 miles away to St. Petersburg, Florida, a bigger city with more opportunities. And she left four-year-old me with my grandmother. It made sense. She couldn't leave a baby with her mother, and I was old enough to be a bit less of a burden to my grandmother. It would be easier for my mother with just the two little ones to care for, rather than three, and she knew I would be in the best hands.

I'm sure my mother discussed it all with her mother. But I haven't dug into that with my mom. Out of respect. But I'd guess that Grandma Mamie was not thrilled with the situation either. Mom and Leroy had been together since she was about thirteen or fourteen.

Mamie must have been thinking, *Oh, Lord, stay away from him. You don't need a boyfriend at this age.*

Then I came along when she was fifteen. People started families early in those days, but still, Mamie must have felt some disappointment.

Mamie would have been supportive of my mother's effort to

fix her life. When it came to me living with her, she must have said something like, *Baby, I got this. You go do what you need to do to make things better. Yes, I got this.*

I have always admired my mother for her courage at this point in her life. She was unhappy with my father and the life they were building, or maybe not building. He was a disinterested parent, unambitious and on his way to becoming an alcoholic. A good time was his priority and would always be. But my mother had grown past that mind-set, and becoming a mother made her realize that there is more to life than dancing, drinking, and carrying on. She wanted to provide a good life for her children, and she understood that it would start with providing a better life for herself.

When she established herself in St. Petersburg, she would send for me. That was her plan and that was what she did. It took her about four years, and rather than feeling left out or abandoned, I look back on those years as a blessing because I spent them with Grandma Mamie, who gave me the foundation of my life.

It was a bold and risky decision but it was the right one. My mother made it the right one through determination and hard work.

I visited my mother and siblings every summer during the years I lived with my grandmother. I always say that I spent about four years living with my grandmother. It might have been less time. In my mom's mind, it definitely was. To be honest, I don't really know the exact amount of time. I remember so much of it that it seems like it could have been ten years. It was a hard time in my mother's life and I don't press her on these details. I thank God for her love and Mamie's love, and I know that it all worked out.

* * *

In the early 1950s, Mamie was able to leave the big farm and get a job in housekeeping at a local hospital. After her husband died in 1953, she moved to the house and small farm where I came to live with her in 1960.

Eventually, she was hired by Dr. Manning, who ran the hospital, to work for his family in his home. She was one hell of a domestic, you can be sure. It might not sound like much, but it was better than pulling a plow. It was a prayer come true.

She began sculpting my spirit and soul on the porch of that house at 2120 Miccosukee Road in Tallahassee, Florida.

I can hear my grandmother walking through that house, bow-legged and strong, making things rattle and shake. The thin, circular crocheted area rugs did little to muffle the impact of her stride. I can hear the kerosene lamp on the table and the porcelain dolls on the shelf shaking as she went from room to room on the thin wooden floors. She was just walking. She was not stomping. But you knew when she was coming. And if her pace was quick, it was all a bit louder and you might want to hide.

My grandmother often told me about the days and times before I came along. As a child, I heard those stories as history, but now I realize she was telling me about herself. She'd say something like:

People used to carry a little stick with them so they were ready when rattlesnakes struck. Yes, I walked with a little stick, too. We used to kill rattlesnakes, but I wasn't afraid of them. That's why I eat everything but rattlesnake.

In one sense, it's a small, exciting story for a little boy to hear about his grandma. Now I think of it as a way to understand her life better. In that scene, I see that her life was hard. She was on the lookout for deadly snakes as a child. I'm not surprised that she killed them, too. She would do what she had to do. Still, no wonder they didn't do much for her appetite. I knew it was true, too, because when I lived with her, we had a guy that would come over to take care of any snakes that got into the house.

I have one strong rattlesnake memory, one that has endured, and it backs up Grandma's story. I was very young, lying in a bed. I don't recognize the room so it must have been before my mother moved to St. Petersburg. I must have still been a baby. I'm looking up and I see this snake on the wall coming down toward me. I'm just looking at it, and then I remember at the last minute, as the snake gets very close to me, my mother runs in, scoops me off the bed, and runs out. My grandmother comes in right behind her with an axe handle. I don't know what happened next but it probably wasn't good for the snake. My mother and grandmother have always been there for me.

Mamie's house on Miccosukee Road had an orange clay driveway. On the left as you drove in and parked, there was a crab apple tree and there were always crab apples on the ground over there. To the left of that tree was a stretch of land that was too big to be a garden but not big enough to be farmland. Mamie grew corn and collard greens there. She had a pomegranate tree, too, and I used to love climbing up the tree and knocking down a few pomegranates and taking them inside to eat.

In front of the driveway, about 300 feet away, there was the outhouse in the backyard. There were trees in the backyard that had Spanish moss, a well-known feature of life in Tallahassee. We weren't too poor to have toilet paper, but we made use now and then of the Spanish moss when using the outhouse.

On the right side of the driveway, there was a small, grass-covered mound that came in from the street. At the end of that stretch of built-up ground were three makeshift brick steps leading to a screen door that went into the house. On the right, there was a porch that was ten feet wide and six feet deep with a small rail along the front. There were always two rocking chairs on the porch, facing out to the road, and behind them were screened windows leading into the small living room.

Stepping into the house, you would be in that living room. My grandma had a couch, a chair, and a couple of tables. Going down the hall, you'd come to her bedroom, and beyond her bedroom was another room with a bed, where I slept when I lived there. There were no doors and she might put up a little cloth or drape to separate the spaces. Farther down the hall, there was the kitchen with its sunken wooden floor. That was the house.

Mamie and I spent a lot of time together on that porch, talking and laughing and just enjoying each other's company. We'd sit on that porch and play games. We'd wait for a car to go by and I'd say, "That's my car, Grandma!" The next one would be hers. I would laugh when my car was a beautiful 1955 Chevrolet and the next one, hers, was an old beat-up truck. In the country, simple things like that are entertaining. She was also teaching me to make the most of my surroundings and to be able to enjoy myself in any setting. We would laugh and laugh, playing "That's my car!" That may be why I love to laugh so much, being exposed to the simple joy of it at such a young age and in such a loving atmosphere.

Grandma would usually be doing something while we spent time on the porch. She'd read the paper and share with me what she was reading. She always read the *Tallahassee Democrat*. She made me curious when she told me stories that I wasn't sure about. I remember one time she said, "Oh, my God! It says right here that a lady was electrocuted while she was vacuuming. Hmmm, hmmm, hmmm!"

I'd say, "Really, Grandma? That's in the paper? Wow!"

"Yes, baby, it says so right here."

She'd read from the Bible, too. She had a very old one whose cover was black in the center but brown around all the edges. Her reading to me inspired me to be a reader so I could find out for myself what was going on.

If she wasn't reading, we'd be shucking beans or corn. With butter beans, you have to take them out of the shell before you cook them. I'd help her with that. Preparing stuff to eat. Other times, I would sit down with her to eat a bowl or a basin full of berries.

My grandmother and I developed an unusual closeness that lasted until she died. She had 55 grandchildren and 125 great-grandchildren. But we had a special connection. I assume it had a lot to do with these early years and all the times when it was just the two of us. We even used the same bathwater.

She would heat the water and pour it in the tin tub in the kitchen. She would take her bath. I'd be in the living room and she'd call out, "I'm done!" Then I would get in that tub, water still warm, and take my bath. When I was finished, I would drag the tub outside, empty the water in the backyard, and hang the tub up on the side of the house.

Mamie's style was very down home. She usually wore a basic housedress, blue or gray, that covered her knees. She wore slippers in the house, not overly feminine either. Just basic bedroom shoes.

When she went out, she loved to wear hats. But no yellow or purple hats. The basic blue, white, or gray would do just fine. Also, when leaving the house, Mamie wore white shoes with thick, wide heels. She liked pocketbooks and had a few different kinds, all in the same simple colors. She liked pink dresses for a little more color, but overall, she was very conservative and straightforward in her appearance. Mamie didn't wear much makeup. She didn't use lipstick either. She wore a pearl necklace and earrings, but nothing striking or out of the ordinary.

There wasn't a lot of going out anyway. She didn't go to parties and we didn't go out to eat because nobody could cook like her. If we did, it would be to a family-style place like Morrison's Cafeteria.

She made her own brown soap, using a country recipe. She had a light scent of vanilla from the soap, like the aroma in the house when she was baking a pound cake. She also had the smell of body lotion, just like my mom does.

As I said, Grandma Mamie was a wonderful cook. I liked everything she made. Macaroni and cheese with some ham. I don't usually eat potato salad but I liked hers. Grandma's best dish was cabbage. I could smell it as she cooked it. She'd put some ham hock or some other pork in with it, a nice combination of meat and vegetable. For dessert, Grandma's banana pudding was the best.

Grandma also loved apple butter, a brown jelly-like spread. She'd buy it and we'd put it on our biscuits at breakfast. She liked to make biscuits and hers were awesome. Along with her coffee, she'd have biscuits, scrambled eggs, and grits for breakfast.

Grandma didn't talk much about Santa Claus. She was a strong, churchgoing Christian so I never really got into the Santa Claus part of it when I was living with her. Later on, when I moved to St. Petersburg to join my mother and the rest of my family, I would hear my siblings talking about how "Santa Claus is going to bring me this and he'll bring you that!" That line didn't work with me and I would say, "There is no Santa Claus. We're buying that stuff. We're paying for it!"

Grandma and I always went out and got a Christmas tree. In the country, you cut down your own tree and brought it home. I liked that ritual and the smell of that pine in the house. If you didn't have a Christmas tree in the house, it didn't feel right.

When I moved in with Grandma, her youngest child, Charles, was there now and then. It was mostly just the two of us, but I remember him coming and going, and I remember when he went off to the military. Grandma had a boyfriend at the time, too. Mr. Nathan. I didn't understand until later. At the time, I just knew he was my grandma's good friend. He would take us for rides in his car, and he was always very kind to me. He'd be there on some mornings, and I put it all together when I was older. And my mom confirmed it.

Grandma Mamie loved having company. It seemed like there was always somebody visiting. Whether it was cousins from down the street or an uncle or aunt visiting Tallahassee, they were welcome at Mamie's house. If there were more than three or four people, she would jump up and say in her country way, *Let me go in the icebox and fix y'all sumptin' ta eat!*

She loved the rituals of gathering and eating and talking. Never enough people around for her. She just knew how to make people feel at home, laughing and telling stories and sharing her great food.

Grandma Mamie didn't really have hobbies because they were a bit of an extravagance on a farm. She loved to work in her yard, hoeing, digging, gardening. She showed me how to use an axe so I could cut wood and help her as much as a little boy could.

When she was working like that, I remember her singing church songs.

Jesus, keep me near the cross,
There a precious fountain
Free to all, a healing stream
Flows from Calv'ry's mountain.
In the cross, in the cross,
Be my glory ever;
Till my raptured soul shall find
Rest beyond the river.

She'd sing when she was working in the house, too. It was very calming. Today, when I fly, I sing that hymn to myself during takeoff and landing. Thank you, Grandma Mamie.

My grandmother was a big presence, and she filled all the space around her. I was amazed at how she could possess a room with no effort. I used to marvel how, at family gatherings, she could just say a few words and get done what she wanted or get the help she needed. Remember, she had thirteen children—seven sons and six daughters—who also had children. When her family got together, it was a few hundred people. But she could say, "Son, come in the house and get me that iron over there." She might say to my mother or one of her other daughters, "Sis, come in here and help me with these potatoes."

But her tone was such that they all knew whom she was talking to without saying a name.

My grandmother was also one who would speak the truth. This is hard for me to say, but she'd look at one of my uncles and say, "Son, give me my purse. Let me have it here. Because that one there is gonna be trouble," referring to one of my cousins. She would say things like that because she had strong intuitive sensibilities about people. She could sense a shifty character, even in her own family. She wanted to protect herself and she spoke up. She'd more than earned the right not to have to pull any punches.

She was like that. She was always a storyteller, and she was always preaching but not in a preachy way. She spoke openly and honestly but never tried to hurt anyone. She told it the way she saw it. Didn't matter if you were her grandson.

More than anything, though, Grandma Mamie was about love

and support. Long before I was born, she was on her knees praying for me and for all of her grandchildren.

"Lord, I hope the world is better for them, that they have better lives.

"I hope they all can have careers and raise beautiful families.

"Lord, give them lives with broad hopes and broad possibilities.

"Let them grow up to be preachers or teachers or doctors.

"Or whatever they want to be."

I went back to find that porch recently. But it and the house were gone. Replaced by an apartment building. And gas stations, convenience stores, and other signs of urban creep. The city had come to the country. Must have been somebody else's prayer but that's OK. Nothing can take away what I learned and felt on that sacred piece of land.

Mamie is in my heart, and so is her house.

II.

St. Petersburg

Sometime in 1964, when I was around eight or nine, my mother was ready to have me join her in St. Petersburg. While I lived with my grandmother in Tallahassee, my mother met and married Johnnie Holtzclaw. They eventually had two kids of their own, my brother Donovan, and later when I was in college, my brother Julian came along. I was the oldest of four growing up, but now I'm the oldest of five. In our culture, we don't use words like "step" or "half" to describe siblings. We were all raised the same way and we are family.

The adjustment was difficult for me. There was a clash of cultures when you compare the quiet, peaceful life I had with my grandmother and the way she raised me to my new life in St. Petersburg. I was now one of four kids instead of being the only one. I was adjusting to seeing my mother every day and *not* seeing my grandmother every day. My mother welcomed me with all of her heart but she was also trying to empower Johnnie, her husband and the new head of our household.

Johnnie was a harsh and strict parent, comfortable spanking us with a belt, the opposite of my grandmother. But I'll give him this: he was consistent. All of us kids got the same treatment. Donovan faced the same rules and punishments that Tony, Jackie, and I did.

"I'm going to respect adults. I'm going to do what adults say. I'm going to tell the truth. I'm going to make mistakes but the adults around me are going to help me as I grow and get socialized into the world."

In Tallahassee, I was nurtured with love and guidance. In St. Petersburg, I was getting yelled at and spanked on a regular basis.

When our stepfather beat us, Tony never showed emotion or resistance. Donovan, Jackie, and I would all weep and shout, "Oh, man! Stop it! Stop!" But Tony would never cry out. He just made a grim face and took the punishment. Eventually, he stopped getting hit because it got no reaction. I learned something about toughness from Tony in those moments. I saw how he went within himself to find what he needed. I tried to do that, too. I also learned that if you don't give people what they want, they try another approach.

Tony had flat feet and he wore special shoes for a while. One time he was trying to run away from a beating from Johnnie and he was clunking along slowly in those heavy, braced shoes. I yelled, "Leave Tony alone! No! No! Hit me." But Tony would have none of that and he stopped and took his beating. Like I said: tough.

As time passed, I figured it out on my own. I learned how to deal with Johnnie and his expectations. I began to figure out what he wanted and gave it to him. I tried never to be late, I got my chores done, and I was respectful. Still got hit now and then but that was Johnnie and his distrustful approach to the world. I couldn't change him.

It was hard but we all made it through.

But sometimes I ran to my mother and said, "Mama, what's up?" And she might say, "OK, Johnnie, that's enough!" for a few weeks. But she was trying to balance things. Johnnie was helping her with three kids from another relationship, after all. She walked the line between knowing that all kids need discipline and realizing that it can be overdone. Kids need protection, too.

When they were both out of the house, I was responsible for the other three. Tony told me recently that I was the best father he ever had. He said I taught him how to play basketball and throw a baseball. Other things, too.

"Don't you remember those corrective shoes I had?" he said. "You taught me how to walk. You gave me the confidence to not care what people said or how they looked at me. You gave me the strength to walk in those things until I didn't need them."

I don't really remember it like that. I remember him having those shoes and all of us laughing at him. But I was in charge when Mom and Johnnie were out or away. I stepped in for them and gave Donovan a bath and cooked and generally kept them in line. Or tried to.

One time my mother went out and told me to keep everyone inside while she was gone. We stayed inside but we played baseball in the house. We were running around and we broke one of my mother's favorite things, a porcelain Lassie doll. We tried to put it back together. With Scotch tape! My mother walks in, sees the doll, and goes over to pick it up. It falls apart in her hands.

Unlike Johnnie, and many others of that generation, my mother didn't dole out physical punishment. But she was so mad. I felt I had hurt her heart. I felt like I had broken something that could not be replaced. I took it really hard. Whenever there was trouble while they were gone, I got punished because I was I charge.

During those years in St. Petersburg, we lived on Eighteenth Street, first at 401 and then at 1034. When I arrived, Johnnie and my mom were renting a house from a black woman named Ms. Mills. It was a bigger place than they could afford to own, and it was about three times bigger than Grandma Mamie's house.

Ms. Mills had a little money and lived up north. She would come down in the winter and stay in the back of the house at 401. I liked her. She enjoyed us kids and took an interest in us, and I remember her as the first person outside the family that cared about us.

The house was on a corner lot, and it had a screened-in porch at the front and had two bedrooms: one for my mom and Johnnie and then one for us. It had a kitchen that led out to a staircase into the backyard, which had some trees and a two-car wooden shack garage. That always surprised me. You're in this wooden house but these stairs were solid concrete. It was jarring for a country boy like me. I was coming from a rural setting but everything about St. Petersburg and Eighteenth Street was urban.

The other great thing was that I was now living in a *neighborhood*. We could run around outside and play and there were houses every twenty yards or so. In Tallahassee, you had to go three miles to get to where my father's family and my cousins lived. It was a long walk to see anybody but not in my new home. More people, more kids, more games to play.

There was a palm tree out front, along with that mango tree in the back, but this was city living. It wasn't crowded but it was much more populated than where I'd been. We stayed at 401 Eighteenth Street for about two more years.

We moved to 1034 but it wasn't a big disruption. Our schools didn't change. We moved because it was a chance for Johnnie and my mom to buy a house and invest in themselves. It was a bit smaller than the rented house but we made it work.

Being in St. Petersburg was good for me in a lot of ways, too. Tallahassee was mostly just me and Grandma Mamie, which was great. As I got a little older, it was nice to be with my siblings and to have regular friends that I saw all the time. But we went to see Grandma every summer, and it was always a fun trip and a great time. When the time approached, I would tell my mom excitedly, "I can't wait to see Grandma Mamie!" She was my special grandma and I loved to tell Jackie, Tony, and Donovan about when I lived alone with her.

Those trips were always a blast for us kids. The six of us would pile into the family car and head north. We always bought used, never new. We'd be in our '57 Buick or '63 Ford. One of our cars was a 1974 Chevrolet Impala, which I later owned. We would fix some fried chicken and eat in the car on the way.

Back then you didn't go on the expressway. We took Highway 19, a two-lane highway, for that 300-mile journey. God bless Johnnie and Mom for doing that all those years. We kids always had fun, but it must have been a test for our parents.

I can still remember when her house would come into view. We'd turn into that driveway and she'd be coming down that little set of stairs to greet us. She'd hug my mom and all of us kids. Johnnie, too. And we'd talk about how much fun we were going to have for the next couple of weeks!

These trips were always very social and family-oriented. I got a chance to reconnect with all of my Tallahassee cousins and family. I would also share with my siblings a little bit of what my life was like when I lived with Grandma. We would go out and pick some pomegranates, plums, and berries and just have fun running around.

I would also see my dad on these summer trips to Tallahassee, although he wasn't in my life very much so there's not a lot to recall. But his sisters were in my life, and I loved them very much.

They lived next door to my mother's sister Elouise, who was married to Major, my dad's best friend. Elouise lived about three miles away from my grandmother. The road to their place was paved, but when you drove up close to their house, it was all dirt. There was a trailer and four or five small houses. It was like a compound, I guess.

My life was full and happy on those summer trips back to Tallahassee. It brought back memories of those early days, but it wasn't just the two of us on that porch anymore. I always felt a little sadness when we would head home. Nothing big but just a touch of heartache to leave her again. But I was happy in my new life with my mom and brothers and sister in St. Petersburg, and I'm sure I was laughing all the way home.

Johnnie worked for the city of St. Petersburg—busting up and replacing sidewalks and other physical labor. He moved up and eventually became a supervisor, staying on the truck and telling other guys to bust up the sidewalk, before retiring. He was doing pretty well at the end of his time there.

He used to bring home special items from work now and then. I particularly liked what we called "welfare cheese." It came in boxes and was supplied by the government to poor families. At work, Johnnie would exchange something with one of those families and bring that cheese home to us. And it was good. I made a lot of cheese sandwiches out of that stuff.

From my perspective, my mother and Johnnie had a good relationship in those early years when I went to live with them. There were times when I heard yelling through closed doors at night, when I was supposed to be asleep. They would be screaming at each other.

A few times, I yelled, "Hey, y'all stop that in there!"

And they'd say, "Go back to bed!"

But there are going to be rough times and arguments in any marriage, especially with a blended family and four kids. That's all it was. They're still together after about fifty years, and my mother is not the kind of woman to stick around a bad situation. She's proven that.

When my mom moved to St. Petersburg, she did what was necessary to take care of her family. She started doing other women's hair in her kitchen to make some money. She worked at a soft water laundry, an industrial setting, that washed sheets for hospitals and hotels. She worked in the rooms where they dried the sheets. Hot, sweaty, exhausting work. My mother can be a little anemic, and I remember hearing that she'd faint a lot while doing that job.

Eventually, she became a dietitian and worked in nursing homes. Perhaps not a dream life, but it was a good Christian life. She had a good husband who loved and supported her, and together they raised five children with love, respect, and dignity. Then again, that *is* a life worth dreaming about. I think my mother found the better life she was looking for when she moved to St. Petersburg and married Johnnie Holtzclaw.

My mother did hair in our kitchen for a long time. The money was important to our family. When black people do their hair, they use curlers and a straightening comb. My mom would put the comb on the stove to get it really hot and then would press the hair with it. One time, I was in there talking to my mom while she was doing some woman's hair. I was in her way and she was motioning me to move with the comb and she accidentally burned my forearm as I tried to figure where she wanted me to go. She got me pretty good.

I look at that scar every day. I use it in my life. I see it and I say, "That's a brand. That's my mother saying, 'I've got to do what I got to do to raise my family.'" It reminds me to ask myself if I'm doing all I can to make my life as good as it can be or to make whatever I am working on as good as it can be.

In my senior year of college, my mother and Johnnie were visiting me in Atlanta. Johnnie said, "I did a lot of things when you guys were growing up that I regret now." After that, I thought, *This guy might be OK.* I went from still thinking he was a bit sketchy to maybe seeing he was actually a good guy.

I needed time and perspective to come to terms with Johnnie. When I was growing up, it was definitely, "I hate this crazy motherfucker! Beating my ass all the time!" I had real anger and resentment for a long time.

Later on, I was able to let go of the anger. When I look back at those times now, I remember that he took on the responsibility for raising three kids that weren't his own. It requires a lot of time and work, and he was there for us. The spanking is not excusable, certainly not today. But it was fifty years ago and life was different.

During elementary and middle schools, sports connected me with Johnnie in a good way. I remember sharing time with him, watching all kinds of games on TV and listening to baseball on the radio. We picked our favorite teams and players together, stuff like that.

I did other things with Johnnie that I look back on fondly. On Thursdays and Fridays, we always went fishing. Johnnie taught me how to saltwater fish in the Gulf of Mexico. We would catch the fish and then I would clean, scale, gut, and bag them. Then Johnnie would sell them to the neighbors. To this day, I don't eat shrimp because that's what we used as bait. But I like fish.

It took a while but I got to a good place with Johnnie and have stayed there.

Johnnie has hung in with my mom for the long haul. And now my mom is the dominant one. She's the strong one running the show. Johnnie is ten years older than my mom, and ten years ago he looked to be on his way out. He was forgetting things and really slowing down. Mom saved him by taking charge.

"OK, Johnnie. We need to get you back to health. I'm going to change your diet. I'm going to get you to the doctor and get you some medicine to help you with your aches and pains. And you're going on a walk with me every day!"

While I don't know the exact details of what she did for Johnnie, I do know that it worked. He has made a clear recovery. He's eighty-eight now and looks to be in better shape than anybody.

My mother's love is a good thing to have.

Tell Me What's Goin' On

As I have moved along in life, I have confronted many seeming contradictions. It's not always easy to negotiate certain moments, especially as you are building your character and working out what kind of person you want to be. The choices you make often indicate who the really important people were in your life.

One such area concerns honesty and telling the truth. We all tell little lies that don't hurt anyone. Some of us tell big lies that can hurt others. And some of us lie easily to work a situation to our advantage.

I was here first! Or, *Mom said I could have the last cupcake!*

But each of us has to eventually choose what our relationship to the truth will be. Will we be straight shooters who rarely stray from the facts? Or will our relationship to the truth be pliable and circumstantial? We find ourselves in an endless variety of situations, and it's all a matter of degree. Most of us have the ability to play with the truth. And you do get to choose if, how, and why you use that ability.

Often, too, the decision to be truthful or not is based on what we think the outcome will be. Am I willing to face the consequences? Or do I need an escape?

When I was about six and living with my grandmother, I asked her if I could go down the road to play with my cousins, Jabbo and Iradell. She said yes but to be back home by five thirty for dinner. She was preparing pork chops, greens, and potatoes for dinner. So off I went.

After playing for about an hour, at five o'clock my aunt Elouise told me to start heading home to make sure I was on time. I said good-bye and went down the road.

Halfway home, I stopped to get some berries off a tree and then I sat down to eat them. I was watching the cars go by without a care in the world. I started walking again and soon found a plum tree. Stopped again to sit and enjoy my latest snack. I was in my own happy little world. And then it hit me. I was going to be late for dinner. I got up and started running.

When Grandma's house came into view, I saw her sitting there with the paper, and I started to wave and call to her.

I was nervous as I approached the house. I didn't know what to say, but I was sure she was going to be mad at me.

"Kenny, you're a little late," said Grandma. "Where have you been?"

"I left Aunt Elouise's house at five o'clock. But I stopped a few times to eat berries and plums. And I was just resting while I ate. I'm sorry. I shouldn't have eaten just before dinner."

"It's OK, baby. Go on in and change your shirt and wash up," she said. "You'll still eat a good dinner. And remember, always tell me the truth like you just did. Tell me what's going on."

I've always remembered that story. How nervous I was that I was in trouble. And how quickly she comforted me. And reinforced the idea of being truthful.

Mamie's way has naturally affected the way I work.

When I begin work on a show, I use the first week or so to get to know people, to see how the cast processes information. I'm looking for who is going to be a problem. Who's going to be the termite? How do I have to communicate with each person?

When I see something troubling early on, I deal with it right away. I probably own some kind of record for letting talent go.

In 1995, while I was artistic director at the Alliance Theatre in Atlanta, I had the privilege to direct the premiere of Pearl Cleage's *Blues for an Alabama Sky*. Phylicia Rashad and Bill Nunn were in the cast, two amazing actors. At the time, Bill was doing just about all of Spike Lee's movies, and Ms. Rashad was just coming off *The Cosby Show*. We were lucky to have such high-profile actors in this new play at our small regional theater.

There was an actor working with Ms. Rashad on a scene that expressed his character's strong feelings for her character. The scene needed to show intimacy between them, but he just couldn't get it the way I wanted it. He just kept disappearing. I had to fix it fast. I told him to be bolder and stronger in the scene. And I let him know it was OK to be a little physical.

"So, Ms. Rashad," I said. "You don't mind if he touches you on the waist or the small of your back?"

"He can do anything; whatever it takes to convey that we're in love."

Still, despite those clear and concise notes, he couldn't do it.

The next day I called him in and said, "Hey, this is not working." He understood and left the production.

Over the years, I've discovered that when I had to let someone go because my instincts were telling me that something was not right, almost every time that person was begging to be released. Somewhere in their bodies, they know it. Even if they want to get upset about being fired, on some level they already know.

Wow. I'm not getting it done, and he sees it.

It pays to be direct and truthful. An actor might be slow to admit he or she is not right for a part and will keep working on the role. But a director has to get right down to it. Time is precious when you are working on a play. Rehearsal time is for improving aspects of a performance and exploring the nuances, not for working on the basics of the role.

Being honest can inspire honesty in others. There have been actors that pushed back. They'll say, "I don't understand what you're trying to do with the play so I don't know if this is going to work for me." And that's not quitting either. That's acknowledging a problem and saving everyone a lot of time and stress.

If I feel we're off on the wrong foot with an actor and I know it needs to be dealt with on the spot, I'll tell the other actors to leave the stage and take a break. I need to talk to the actor in question alone. It's a little upsetting and nerve-racking. And sometimes when the cast comes back, I'll tell them we'll be replacing that actor.

I'd bet that most people I've worked with would say, "Oh, he's raw. He's brutally honest. He gets right to it." And that's true. I am an ordinary guy, basic, and down to earth. I don't get into impressing people with my experience and awards or whatever. I don't try to persuade people to my position when it comes to directing. I learned that from my mother when discussing the Bible.

I tell them what I want in many instances, though I encourage individual creativity, too. I'm a country boy from Florida who knows honesty, truth, and what seems real when it's in front of him. And I'm going to tell you the truth about what I see.

Being honest, open, and straight shooting has served me well not only when I'm letting someone go but also when I am giving notes about a performance. My approach, to the famous and the not-so-famous, is always the same: "We're just having a conversation. I'm going to tell you the good and the bad. This is what I love and this is what's not working." And all good actors want to get better. They're open to you when they know you only seek to help and improve what they are doing. The good ones, every time out, want to be the best they can be.

Far from resenting the feedback, they want and demand it. When I give actors truth and honesty from the very beginning, they see it and respect it. I was working on *The Mountaintop* with Sam Jackson for a Broadway run. Early on I told him, "I just don't feel Dr. King's humor in that opening scene, and we need it."

Sam's a strong personality and a dedicated craftsman. He said, "What do you mean?"

And I went on to explain the X, Y, and Z of it as I watched the performance. My comments were truthful and in line with my vision for the play that I had already communicated to Sam and the whole cast.

Sam knows I have no agenda other than what is best for him and the play. What's best for him and the play is his ability to give the best performance he can give. So he listened to my thoughts, took them in, and adjusted what he was doing a little bit. And we moved on to the next scene.

My style of being honest with actors actually starts in the casting process. I met Denzel Washington when we were beginning work on *Fences* in 2011. We met to see if we would like each other. We talked about the play and how we approach our work. We hit it off in that conversation and never looked back. I never faked anything or did anything calculated to win him over. I showed him who I am and what I wanted to do with the play. Honesty works.

Some situations call for an audition. You bring them in and they read with the people you've already cast.

For Joshua Jackson in *Children of a Lesser God*, we did a workshop to hear the play out loud. In those scenarios, you're actually testing each other. He's seeing if he likes the project, and you are seeing if it moves the way you want it to move. That one worked out well, too.

There are many ways to build a cast for a show. But honesty, truth, and a clear vision have to be there from the start. That way, when problems arise, you have a basic premise from which to make a decision on whether a change is necessary. Then you simply go with your gut and tell the truth as you see it.

All these interactions are handled with calm and ease, given to me by my grandmother on that porch in Tallahassee all those years ago.

You Gotta Do Watcha Gotta Do

Many years ago, while I was dating my future wife, Jennifer Thompson, we attended a family Christmas party. She struck up a conversation with my dad. Later she would tell me he said, "I've done more for other kids than I've done for my own."

He was right.

My dad was a pretty loud and boisterous guy. He loved to laugh. That comment to Jennifer was a brief insight, a rare moment of quiet regret. At the time he said it, I was well into adulthood. I think he was trying to say, *I wanted to love him in my way, but when I look at it, I did more for others than I did for my own son. My way didn't really work out.* It didn't affect me one way or the other to hear that he said that. It was just his way of expressing something I already knew.

Leroy never sent us money on our birthdays or holidays. He didn't send cards or call us either. He never sent money to my mother to help raise us, and he certainly didn't help with college. He just didn't have that kind of mentality, to feel the obligation to support his children. It wouldn't have been very hard for him to do more for other kids than his own.

During my childhood, we wouldn't see him for stretches of time that could last as long as a year. When we went back to Tallahassee to visit family for a few days, we would see him each day for an hour or two. That's it. He didn't take us out to eat or to a planned outing to an amusement park. There was never a sense of him going out of his way because his children were visiting, never a sense that it was special or important to him.

About the only thing I can recall from those childhood visits to Tallahassee when I would see my dad is that he would drive, a car or a truck, about 100 miles per hour on Miccosukee Road. As a kid, I'm thinking, *This is great! He's going a hundred!* It didn't occur to me how dangerous that was, but that was Leroy. Having a good time, above all else.

My dad was also a functioning alcoholic. If you met him and he'd had a few, you wouldn't know he had a problem. He didn't overdo it so he could always handle himself well. But he needed that chemical support to feel right.

When I was about forty, I asked him how long he'd been drinking. I was just curious, because every time I saw him, he was either getting ready for a drink or had just had one.

"Since I was one."

I started to laugh but quickly realized he was serious. That was his way of saying he couldn't remember when he didn't drink. And if you ever saw him when he hadn't been drinking, you would know he was an alcoholic. The buzz, the high from alcohol, was essential to his existence. He wasn't himself without it.

When I graduated from college, I invited all my family to Atlanta and I treated everybody to dinner at a nice restaurant. There were about thirty of us, and after we had some hors d'oeuvres, we sat down to eat. But Leroy got right up and walked out. People noticed and were commenting. I followed him out and met him on his way back in.

"What happened, man?" I said. "Where'd you go?"

"I went out to my car for a drink," he said. "I have a little pocket inside my stomach and I have to fill it. And once I fill that pocket, then I can eat."

Leroy wasn't telling me anything that I didn't know. But that moment gave me a deeper understanding about his problem. And I remember feeling appreciative that God kept me away from that problem, of depending on filling up that little pocket.

That story has stayed with me. As a functioning alcoholic, he saw the world that way. He had to fill that pocket before he could do anything. Eat, sleep, work, watch a ball game, whatever. Everything started with filling that little pocket. He was not a falling-down drunk, but he filled that pocket every day. When he went to the car, he drank some Seagram's gin, which comes in a bottle that has little bumps, bars, and knots on the outside surface of the glass. In the black community, it's called knottyhead because of the bottle and what it does to your high. It makes you feel like there are knots inside your head. It's good when you want to get drunk. The bottle isn't smooth and neither is the buzz.

Unlike Leroy, I have something in me that allows me to stay aware when I drink. When I'm having the drink before the one that would get me drunk, it registers with me and I slow down and then stop. I never have that next drink. I like to drink but I don't ever want to be drunk again. God has kept me from the scary, addictive parts of drinking. I am able to stop myself before it gets out of hand. The same impulse kicks in with anything that can be tempting to overdo. Discipline and self-control.

Leroy had his "pocket," and he lived with it as best he could. I saw his condition and took steps not to develop one of my own.

My mother and Johnnie helped me out, too. They didn't drink and I wasn't allowed to have alcohol in the house until after I went to college. By then, Tony and I were drinking Heineken. I would ask my mom if I could put some beer in the refrigerator while I was visiting. She'd say yes, figuring that I was old enough now to make my own decision about drinking and because she had seen that I was being responsible about it.

Despite his shortcomings, Leroy was happy-go-lucky and easy to be around. He liked to laugh and he knew how to enjoy life. But as I've said, he didn't know what being a father was all about. The distance between us in my childhood was his doing. But later in life, we were not ever able to get closer because my path was so very different from anything he knew or could understand.

I remember one time I called him and said, "Hey, man, I got a Broadway show. My first Broadway show. Up here in New York."

And he says, "Well, ya gotta do watcha gotta do!"

His reaction stunned me. He couldn't relate at all to what I had told him. He had no idea of the significance of one of the most important moments in my life. I might as well have told him that I had bought some pants. Our entire relationship was summed up in one moment.

I don't think my dad ever really thought my mom would leave him in Tallahassee and begin a new life in St. Petersburg without him. I think he would have gotten back together with her if he could have. But he went on with his life.

One day my phone rang.

"Hey, man, is this Kenny?"

"Yeah."

"This is your brother."

"My brother? Who are you?"

"Tony."

"Tony who?"

"Tony Leon."

For a long time, Leroy dated a woman named Mary, and they had kids. She was pretty with dark skin and long, black hair.

This was Leroy's son from that relationship. He named the kid Tony, despite already having a son named Tony. And that was how I found out.

Leroy never came to me and explained it. I confronted him.

"Why didn't you tell me? What happened here?"

"Well, her favorite name is Tony," he said. "I figured they would never meet or see each other."

Due to my father's unique relationship to parenting, I have two brothers named Tony Leon. That really does sum up Leroy as a father.

I always liked Leroy's family. They were all good people. His parents were my grandfather Zack and my grandma Alice. I vaguely remember spending time with them as a young boy in those years I lived with my grandmother. I even met my great-grandmother Lena, who was the oldest person I knew as a child. Zack Leon smoked a pipe and I loved the sweet smell of his tobacco. We used to go outside and play in this old, abandoned 1950 Chevy he had on blocks in his backyard. We'd go and sit in there and pretend we were driving.

I loved my father's sister Veda Mae. We called her Tiny and she was fun-loving and down to earth. I saw her whenever I could and always enjoyed being with her. She took so much pride in everything I did, and she would share my career progress with that side of the family.

"Kenny is doing great! He's directing all these plays and movies!"

I was always touched that she cared so much and wanted to have a connection with me and Tony. We stayed in touch and always checked in with her when we were in Tallahassee, especially as she dealt with cancer at the end of her life.

One time, when she had less than a year to live, I told her about a play I was directing in Atlanta.

"I wanna come see it!" she said.

We kept talking and it sank in that I would not be onstage.

"Wait! You're not in it? Oh, I don't want to see that!"

At my grandmother's funeral, I got a little insight into my childhood days. I had always romanticized them as mostly being just her and me and she was the one who took care of me. I also remembered spending time with my mother's sister Elouise, whom I love to this day. But a few older ladies at Mamie's funeral said, "I'm Miss So-and-So. You stayed with us for a little while in those years." I found out there were a few other people that loved on me as a child. It was mostly my grandmother, but she had a little help from both my mother's and my father's families and some neighbors.

There was a void left by my father's lack of interest in being a dad. But I was lucky because the void was filled by so many people who loved me. I turned out all right because I got the support and love every child needs, from family and friends. Because of that, I never harbored any hatred or resentment toward my father. We had the best relationship that we could have. He loved me in his way, and I accepted him on the terms that he chose. We laughed a lot together, and many children get far less.

Leroy Leon died in 2015, at age seventy-eight, after multiple strokes.

My full name is Kenneth Leroy Leon. I bear my father's name. Phylicia Rashad once told me that my name means "Handsome lion king." Kenneth means "handsome," Leon is "lion," and Leroy means "the king."

Handsome lion king, that's me. And my dad is part of me.

Rest in peace, Leroy.

You, too, Tiny.

Sweet Potato Pie

Like her mother, my mother is also a resourceful and sometimes magical cook, who can make feasts out of what you might call scraps or leftovers. Some ham, collard greens, cole slaw, potato salad, macaroni and cheese. But when you cook with love and for loved ones, those are not scraps or leftovers. Those things are the starting point for an opportunity to share a meal and enjoy some time together. Maybe the food makes the time together so sweet. Maybe the time together makes the food taste so good. The best thing to do is savor every moment. And every bite.

When I was growing up with Mom, Johnnie, and my siblings, Sunday was always our best meal. On Sunday, you're talking about fried chicken, collard greens, macaroni and cheese, corn-bread. Everybody could have their choice of what they wanted to drink, whether that was a Coke, 7UP, water, or Kool-Aid. We were big on those Kool-Aid packs; we'd pick the flavor, put the pack of mixture in water, add sugar, stir it up, and add ice. Sunday meals also had a nice dessert—sweet potato pie or banana pudding. Those Sunday meals were great.

My mother has always made wonderful food for me and my siblings. But above all, I treasure her sweet potato pie, often the star of our big Sunday dinners. I learned to love it from a young age, and later in life, she would make me four or five to take back to my dorm. When those ran out, she would bake even more and send them to me.

When those pies arrived, it felt like I was home. Especially when I was homesick as a freshman. I might be feeling a little blue and then those pies would be there to pick me up. It was like getting a little piece of Mom in college, very comforting. And it wasn't just me that loved those pies. Ron Williams, a New Jersey guy, and James Green, my roommates, would perk up when they saw me come in the room with my mail.

"Oh, Kenny, did your mom send some pies?"

"Yes, she did! Let's dig in!"

And I'm not in her house more than ten minutes now before I ask, "Mom, you got any sweet potato pie?" She usually does. Well, until I eat it all.

Of course, there are many things in this life that bring her to my mind. But her sweet potato pie does it best. The warm, rich taste and smell of the cinnamon and butter she uses in the recipe never fail to brighten my day and lighten my load. And that pie reminds me of all the wonderful family meals we had growing up.

My mother can cook wonderful meals from the best fish, chicken, beef, vegetables, fruits, and greens. She's now the kind of cook who can shop for what she wants, bring it home, and whip up something amazing. She doesn't need a cookbook or a recipe unless she's just read something that piques her interest. But she has so many reliable meals to make that she usually sticks with them. When I ask my mother what she's preparing, no matter what she says, I'm happy. I know it will be good. I only ask out of curiosity and so I can get my taste buds ready.

My grandmother, and my mother, amazed me in so many ways. They were both so resourceful. They both knew how to make a lot out of a little. I'm sure my mother smiles at the memory of baking me so many sweet potato pies. An easy, almost effortless, task for her that had, and has, such a profound effect on me. True and complete nourishment. That's why they call it soul food.

So, yes, I will share with you a recipe for sweet potato pie.

But not just any sweet potato pie.

My mother's sweet potato pie.

Note: If you're going to bake this, and I encourage you to, remember that this is just a recipe. These are the things my mother uses to make her pies. The most important ingredient is you. There is a lot of leeway here for taste (sugar, nutmeg, lemon, cinnamon) and for your take on when it's "done." This recipe is a place to start. You may need to make it many times before you find what works for you and your loved ones. And you'll never catch my mom! But when you find you have mastered this soulful recipe, you'll be glad you did. And you'll have another go-to dish for your family's ongoing menu.

Before you warm up the oven, I'll say to you what my mother and grandmother have always said to me, in so many ways, over the years: Put your touch on it. And the people who love you will love your food.

ANNIE RUTH HOLTZCLAW'S SWEET POTATO PIE

6 large sweet potatoes
2 sticks butter
4 eggs
¼ cup milk
2 tablespoons vanilla flavor
½ teaspoon lemon flavor
2 tablespoons flour
1 teaspoon cinnamon
½ teaspoon nutmeg
Sugar to taste

Boil and peel the potatoes. Blend to remove the strings. Add all the other ingredients and blend together to your taste and sweetness.

Note: Not all potatoes are the same so adjust the amounts of the ingredients to your taste and the size of the potatoes.

Put the mixture in a pie shell and bake at 350 degrees until done, about 30 to 40 minutes.

Tony, Jackie, Donovan, and Julian

Grandma Mamie and my mother have taught me many lessons through their words and actions. My priorities, my values, are a blend of what they've shown me and what my life experiences have taught me. Family is very important, especially the relationship between generations. But I also treasure my own generation: Tony, Jackie, Donovan, and Julian. We have the same beautiful woman as our mother. We were also all raised by Johnnie Holtzclaw. We have much in common, though our paths in life have been quite different. We are accepting of our differences, and we love each other in our own ways.

Grandma Mamie had nearly 200 grandchildren and great-grandchildren. And we all think we were her favorite. I certainly do. But Grandma didn't have favorites. She wanted the same thing for all of us: a better life.

Grandma Mamie's descendants are all over the country now. We've taken her spirit with us to New Jersey, New York, Georgia, as well as Florida.

Just as Grandma Mamie was, I am very proud of my brothers

and sister. I don't know a better person than Tony Leon. People quickly come to love Tony because he's an authentic person. He's honest and true. And he's very skilled with his hands. If he sees something broken in your house, he'll fix it free of charge. He got that from Grandma, that sense of generosity and giving.

I see Grandma in how Jackie has overcome life's challenges and remained a loving and caring soul.

I see Grandma in how Donovan found his calling early and has gone from being a security guard to being in charge of the setup of conventions at the World Congress Center in Atlanta.

Julian has struggled to find a good path in his life, but he's put it all together recently and is in a good place. Through it all, he had a good spirit and always cared about other people. When I see that side of him, I see Grandma.

I believe that Tony, Jackie, Donovan, and Julian are the products of generational prayers just as I am. They are all sweet, kind, beautiful people that I would love even if they weren't related to me. When I see their essential goodness at work, when I see how loving and nurturing they are, I see Grandma Mamie. All of us would not be who we are without her spiritual gifts and her prayers.

Upward Bound

In the mid-to-late 1960s, St. Petersburg was divided roughly along racial lines. The south side of town was black, and the north side was white. I went to Sixteenth Street Junior High School in 1967 and 1968, and I was looking forward to attending Gibbs High School in the fall of 1969. Gibbs was a mostly black school and an athletic powerhouse that delivered a sense of pride to the community. But I never made it to Gibbs.

St. Petersburg was not immune to the racial tensions that had a hold on the United States in those years. Integration was a common urban public policy at the time, and by my freshman year in high school, busing was in full bloom in the service of racial equality. School buses in St. Pete took black kids from their south side communities and divided them up among six different, mostly white, high schools on the north side. I ended up at Northeast High School.

Northeast served one of the wealthiest white communities in the state, and the school was filled with amenities unheard of on the south side. It had an elaborate driver education program,

60

with a special practice course that had stop signs and traffic lights. Many of the students drove motorcycles to school, and there was a whole section of the parking lot dedicated to those bikes. The transition to this school was jarring for all the kids on those buses, including me. It was all so foreign, and it was so much better than what we had. They had computers; we had books. They had five swimming pools; we had one or none. It was still St. Pete but it was not our St. Pete. When we got older, some of us got cars, but during those first two years, we rode the bus, from our community to theirs.

The school was on a modular schedule with the day divided up into twenty-minute chunks. You could have a class for two or three mods. You also could have many mods of free time each day, as much as eighty minutes in a row. But if you were away from your home neighborhood, what good was it? Just the idea of free time in the school day was odd to us. We ended up going to the library, hanging around the campus, or going across the street to shoplift.

Early on, there were race riots and confrontations going on everywhere in the country. The early 1970s was a time of protest, and Northeast High had its share. This was the time of streakers and other forms of civil unrest. There were protests against the Vietnam War, but we had our own reasons, too. We didn't want to be there, and they didn't really want us there. We resented these rich kids, and I had friends who would throw these white kids' bikes and motorcycles into the school swimming pools. The white kids hated us.

Northeast did have several teachers, black and white, who

really cared about the students and wanted to make sure we made the transition as well as possible. I remember Mr. Felton, a black counselor, especially being concerned and doing all he could to help us navigate this big, sudden change in our lives.

The tension was everywhere at school. In the theater program, they would only consider black kids for roles like maids, butlers, and chauffeurs. You couldn't play a politician or a teacher or a lawyer. You couldn't even play yourself. As a result, I boycotted theater.

Still, I was a guy who believed in coming together and over-coming differences. I was looking to make friends and figure out this new place. My mother and my grandmother would not have put up with us getting in trouble anyway. I knew I had to be part of the solution. I'd never been taught hate anywhere I lived, and I'd had a lot of spiritual training. We're all God's children, and we're all here together on this planet. Better to be friends than enemies.

My best friend was Marshall Lester, who was the top basketball player in the state. I wasn't that good at basketball but I hung around with the team because of Marshall. I eventually made a lot of white friends, including Craig Pippin, another basketball player. He reminded me of Pete Maravich with his fancy skill set and behind-the-back passes. Craig and his sister Sharon were good friends of mine, and I got to know them well. The Pippins were a great family that embraced blacks easily and warmly. Hanging out with them showed me the way the world could and should be. I've lost touch with the Pippins, and they may not even know how much they inspired me.

I played sports with other white kids and eventually found a way to fit in and even become a leader that people looked to for guidance.

By my junior year, things had gotten much better. Time passed, people adjusted, and the tensions simmered down. In school, I was trying to talk to both black and white kids about ways to make it work. I would bring them together for meetings after school. I always saw myself as some kind of a political/ministerial leader. I enjoyed the challenge because I thought the goal, a calmer, safer school environment, was worthwhile. I was eventually elected student council president.

By my senior year, I knew one thing: after integrating a white high school and learning about how to get along better with white people, I needed to go to a historically black college or university, an HBCU as they are called. I might not have felt that way had I gone to Gibbs, but I definitely wanted to get in touch, as an older person, with my black heritage, roots, and culture. Fours years of being in a kind of "white" world made me feel like I needed to reexamine and get to know my own people in a deeper way.

When I was a freshman at Northeast, I got involved with the Upward Bound program, which is a federally funded college preparatory program for students from low-income families that have college potential. I went to classes every Saturday during the school year, and I spent summers staying at a dorm and studying at Eckerd College in St. Petersburg. Angela Bassett was in the program with me, and we remain friends to this day.

In Upward Bound, we competed athletically and academically

against other Upward Bound programs throughout the state. We got thorough college preparation in math, science, the arts, and sports. We competed in basketball and bowling, and we competed through the plays we were in as well. There was also social training because we met and competed with other students from across Florida.

There was a counselor in St. Petersburg named Sevelle Brown, not affiliated with Northeast High School, who recruited kids from all the high schools, especially after integration and busing had started. It was a major turning point in my life to join Upward Bound. No one in my family had gone to college, and my family did not have much money. But Upward Bound prepared me academically, along with my regular high school work, to have a shot at continuing my education.

Not only did Upward Bound prepare me with my studies, but the program also helped me navigate the application process to any school that my scores and grades supported. This part of the process was important to me because I had decided I wanted to go to an HBCU but I didn't really know that much about them.

The closest HBCU was Florida A&M but that was in Tallahassee. With all the family I had there, it would not have felt like I was getting away and moving on, which was also important to me at the time. I wanted to get out of Florida if I could, to see and experience another part of the country. Just as my mother knew she had to get out of Tallahassee, I knew in my bones there was more for me than St. Petersburg. I knew I was getting out of there. I just didn't know exactly where I was going.

The next state over was Georgia so I looked into that with my

Upward Bound counselors. They told me that Atlanta had a lot of black schools.

"Tell me about them," I said.

"Well, Spelman is all girls. Morehouse is all guys. And Clark College is coed."

"Coed? I'm on that! Let's apply there!"

I went to visit the school and to see Atlanta. It was everything I was looking for—a big, international city, away but not too far away from home, and a very good school. I got in.

Atlanta, and Clark College, here I come.

I will carry those Upward Bound people and experiences in my heart forever. That program showed me a way to improve my life and to expand my horizons. Not only did I make lifelong friends in Upward Bound, but I feel as though that time gave me a little edge that I could draw on when I needed it.

Not to get overly political, but this country got two hundred years of free labor from black people. That's a fact. Black people have played a major role in making this country as beautiful as it is. And despite their contributions, generation after generation of black people in America did not get an education and were not allowed to worship God as they wished. All of that took a toll, and it is only fair for that inequity to be addressed in some way. Upward Bound provided an opportunity for minority and underprivileged kids to play catch-up so that we would have an equal opportunity for success in this country that our ancestors helped to build. Just as this country owes a lot to Native Americans, this country owed a program like Upward Bound to black Americans. I will always support that kind of program.

My grandmother did not have anything like Upward Bound when she was young. Her grandmother's life lacked so much that she couldn't even read. I always feel gratitude for those who came before me. I owed it to Grandma Mamie to take advantage of things that could help me prosper and grow. I had to do my part to let her prayers for me come true. I knew I had to work to get the better life she wanted for me.

Without Upward Bound, I don't know where I'd be today. I would not be directing plays for the stage and television. I would not have gone to college, that's for sure. I knew that country road in Tallahassee and that small house in St. Petersburg, and I'd seen a bit of the wider world in books and magazines and on television. But I had no idea how to get out into that world.

Upward Bound gave me an edge that became a foundation to build my dreams on. All of that work I put in, all of that exposure to other people from across the state, the college counseling all came together to make me stronger and to give me a chance to compete for success in this world. Upward Bound showed me that success is related to effort, and that work ethic has been invaluable to me ever since.

I get annoyed when people refer to programs like Upward Bound as handouts that don't work. Upward Bound gave me a path to travel on, but I had to do the work and put in the time. I went to school six days a week and in the summer. Nobody handed me anything. I know of many examples besides myself of kids whose lives were forever improved simply because they got a chance to help themselves. Upward Bound gave me the chance my grandmother never had. I was not about to waste it.

III.

Mr. Irresistible

My four years at Clark College were pretty typical college years. I learned and grew a lot, made a lot friends, had a lot of fun. With my family's limited finances, I had to be pretty resourceful to pay for it. But I got by on a combination of loans, work-study, and scholarship money.

I was looking to expand my horizons and learn more about my own heritage and culture. It paid off pretty quickly. I met Maynard Jackson during freshman orientation. He was running for mayor and ended up winning. I was fortunate to meet him when I did because I was looking for role models and he was the first black mayor of Atlanta. We became friends and he was an informal mentor. When he passed in 2003, his wife asked me to speak at his funeral. I read his favorite poem, "Determination" by Ella Wheeler Wilcox.

The opening lines still speak to me today:

There is no chance, no destiny, no fate,
Can circumvent or hinder or control
The firm resolve of a determined soul.

My school life led me to meet other black people, like bankers and lawyers. And then I saw Spelman College, which has thousands of black women from all over the world. The world was opening up.

All of my friends were in the Omega Psi Phi fraternity, and they pledged at the same time. I was involved in other things on campus, so by the time they wanted me to pledge, I wasn't interested. Pledging a frat can be nasty business, and I didn't want to join that badly.

Just as in high school, I was always trying to be aware politically and socially. I wanted to contribute to the community. One day I was talking to some sorority girls from Delta Sigma Theta.

"Kenny, we need to get the guys involved more on campus," they said. "But we don't know how. We're going to have this competition called Mr. Irresistible. If you signed up, the others guys would fall in line because you're so popular."

I figured, *What the hell?*

So I entered what was essentially a beauty contest. I'm up there in a bathing suit, very short black briefs really. I'm answering questions.

They asked me, "Who are your role models?" This was about 1974 or so.

I said, "Muhammad Ali and Richard Pryor." That remains a great answer. Their strong beliefs, their humor, the way they lived their lives, all still admirable. Add Dick Gregory, too.

Turned out to be the right answer, too, because I won. There were two results from that contest: One, it actually did bring the student body together and got the guys to be more involved going forward. And two, I still get teased about it today.

Hey, there's Kenny Leon, the first Mr. Irresistible at Clark College!
For most of college, I had a steady girlfriend. We were Kitty and Kenny. People thought we would eventually get married. We didn't but we had fun. She was from Jamaica and she always went around barefoot. That caught my eye and we ended up dating. I liked her because she had a freedom and spontaneity about her. You should have seen us walking around campus, this guy walking around with a big Afro and this smaller woman in jeans and bare feet. Kitty was also an actor and we shared that, too. We drifted apart years after college but our friendship endured to the point that I am godfather to one of her daughters.

I met Samuel Jackson; his eventual wife, LaTanya Richardson; and Bill Nunn while I was an undergrad. There was limited black professional theater in Atlanta at that time so all of the semiprofessional theater happened at Clark. That was how the professionals worked with us students, and we would do plays at school and other parts of Atlanta.

When I was in college, I had a theater instructor named Joan Lewis, who was really hard to please, very challenging, and intense. We worked on legitimate, classic plays.

I took a handful of classes from Joan but acted in eight or nine plays for her, and she was a hands-on drill sergeant, a screaming, smart, wise, and crazy demander of *Truth!* Professionals like Sam Jackson would play a role for six performances, and students like myself would play that role for one performance—a real learning situation. Sometimes Joan would rehearse us all night long, working us from 5:00 p.m. to 8:00 a.m. the next day.

Also, during the summers of my college years, I participated in

Atlanta Street Theatre. Run by Michelle Rubin, it was a program funded by a grant from CETA (Changing Education Through the Arts), a federally sponsored initiative that provided jobs in the arts in inner-city neighborhoods. Every summer we would make up plays for elementary school kids, and it gave them a good introduction to improv, acting, and performance. I got paid, and that's where I first learned the improvisation techniques that I would develop more deeply in my years at the Academy Theatre.

Barbara Jones taught me economics at Clark, and it was eye-opening for me. Being from a humble background, I was fascinated by trends and theories about money, markets, and business.

When I was at the Academy of Theatre and Music, I pursued a master's degree and studied with Mack Jones, Barbara's husband. Mack had this program in which you studied economics, politics, and sociology, but everything was from the point of view of being black in America. For instance, how does the electoral college affect African Americans? We also studied other countries such as Cuba and many African nations.

The Joneses were very influential teachers for me. Their courses were exciting and provocative because they both had a way of talking about any subject and making it real and personal. You'd take their lessons and see how they fit into your life, your decisions, and your plans.

Today, whenever I can, I go to my True Colors Theatre Company and greet people on their way out of the theater. One night, I looked up and here come Drs. Barbara and Mack Jones to shake my hand, and getting the chance to thank them in person was so meaningful for me. Their classes taught me everything I would need to know to do theater as I have. Much like Grandma Mamie, they helped me see myself in the world. They showed me how to be productive based on where and how I grew up. I've always retained a snapshot of them in my mind. They said they were proud of me. And I told them I would never have done what I've done without their direction and their excellence as educators.

Carol Mitchell

I met Carol Mitchell when I was an undergraduate at Clark College and she was in the graduate program at Atlanta University. We had many friends in common, we read the same books, and we shared a love of theater—acting, directing, and teaching.

Carol was a wonderful actress, and I loved working with her. During my time in college, we were very good friends, exceptionally close, like brother and sister. I knew I could trust in her support and advice as I was trying to figure out life and she could do the same with me. We saw each other's plays and worked alongside each other on various projects, and we sustained that closeness all the way through.

After our time at Clark and Atlanta, while I was working out my next step, Carol got a job at my future home, the Southeastern Academy of Theatre and Music. She was one of the first African Americans to work there. She worked in the Children's Theatre and acted.

In those days, and later, people were always curious about us.

We used to talk about it in college, how people would ask us if we were dating.

"Oh, no!" we would say.

"I would never date him," she would add.

We didn't think we were right for each other. In fact, she would try to hook me up with other women for dates. We had a closeness that was undeniable but there was no spark or romance.

I Will Not Do the Bidding
of the Man!

After college, I went to Southwest University School of Law in Los Angeles. That was just the next step on the path I was traveling. I had gathered some momentum in this direction, I suppose, but some part of me knew that I really didn't want to be a lawyer. I headed to LA a bit restless and unsure. I planned to take it seriously, of course, but something nagged at me that I couldn't quite figure out. It wasn't so much that I knew I didn't want to be a lawyer. It was more that I really didn't have a clear sense of what I truly wanted. I went to law school because I didn't have anything better or more promising to do, like many students who find themselves in law school.

However, two things happened to me while I was in Los Angeles that brought things into focus and helped me sort out this part of my life.

In my first few months in Southern California, I dealt with some racism, in a weird, subtle way. I had housing problems where I was staying because the landlord did not know I was black. He rented to me assuming I was white because there weren't a lot of black people at my law school. It's not like he mistreated me, but it was clear that my skin color mattered. You get looks, you know? I knew LA would be different from Atlanta, but this was too much.

The other factor was also a bit vague but also real. I did not like the social vibe in Los Angeles. I'm from the South. I'm accustomed to walking down the street and politely greeting people with some eye contact, a smile, and a kind word.

"Hello, what's up? Nice day, huh?"

You don't really expect an answer, but you usually get one back with a nice nod or whatever. It's a quick, friendly, welcoming social transaction. It's part of what is known as Southern hospitality.

But I found if I said that to a stranger in LA, they'd stop and say curtly, "Do I know you?"

They were waiting for the follow-up. *Do you have more to say to me? If not, why did you speak to me in the first place?* I found that aspect of the culture weird and cold. It's funny that I ended up working in an industry with a huge presence in Los Angeles. My first brush with the city did not go well at all.

While I was in law school and dealing with a city I couldn't get comfortable in, back in St. Petersburg five of my best friends were in a serious car accident. One of them, Greg Stokes, was dating my sister Jackie at the time and would later be the father of her first child. They ran their car off the road, flipped it, and landed on a golf course. It was very serious. They weren't supposed to survive.

It was enough to get me to leave Los Angeles and law school at the same time. I wasn't happy where I was and my friends needed me. It all added up to me heading back home.

I got to St. Pete, and as it turned out, they were all going to make it. Greg had permanent spine damage and was never really the same person afterward. But he was alive and so were the others.

Once that situation became less dire, I looked around and did some thinking. I had withdrawn from law school and couldn't return for a year. So how was I going to spend that time?

It was definitely the right move for me to go back to St. Pete for my friends. But I could not stay there for twelve months. Now I was back where I went to high school, and I was in the culture of that part of Florida. I loved to visit there but college had changed me. I had experienced the international flavor of Atlanta, the power and inspiration of an African American mayor, meeting and getting to know all kinds of women and men from all over the world. St. Pete felt small compared to all of that excitement and opportunity.

And as much as I loved my family, I had to go with my head and my heart. They both told me to go to Atlanta.

I did the paperwork to return to law school the following year, then I found myself in Atlanta with a year on my hands. I needed a job.

For a while, I did undercover security work. Snitching on people at various job sites. I did it for about half a year but eventually quit. It was not for me.

I Don't See You as a Director

At this time, the fall of 1979, I'd been doing a lot of starting and stopping. Law school and Los Angeles then suspending those studies to go back to St. Pete. Then off to Atlanta. Undercover job and then unemployed. Looking back, I realize two things. First, these were early examples of me trying to heed my grandmother's and mother's advice to be true to myself and to trust my instincts and guts, to be wary of big compromises. I was beginning to see their wisdom in practical, real-life settings. Those situations were not right for me, and they hounded me until I fixed them.

Second, I see now that I had a real interest in the theater because of how I'd spent my time in college. But I don't think I yet believed anyone could make a living doing theater. That belief was about to be tested.

After quitting the snitch gig, I saw an article in the paper about actor auditions for the Academy of Theatre and Music. They were looking to diversify their company and were specifically looking for African Americans. My gut told me to go after this intriguing opportunity. And I figured I had enough experience to give it a try.

When I auditioned for the Academy Theatre, it wasn't like I was completely new to that world. I drew on what I'd learned working in college with Joan Lewis and Michelle Rubin in my audition and interviews. And they took me. It all happened pretty fast.

Still known today as the Academy Theatre, this organization was right up my alley. They were very socially conscious and interested in community outreach, ideas central to what I do now in all my work. The theater's founder, Frank Wittow, ran a demanding company and really pushed us all to learn and grow together. You could be acting in *Hamlet* or *Death of a Salesman* at night and be doing workshops in prisons in the daytime.

Another point of emphasis was improvisation. We would make up scenes on the spot using improvisational techniques, putting together plays as ideas came to us in the moment.

Improvisation allows you to use the five senses to slow down time in a way and act on top of the lines. Improv teaches you to engage the entire body in an effort to be alive moment to moment. Improvisation was and is the backbone of everything I do for live theater.

So, with the emphasis on creativity in the moment and the social commitment, I quickly felt right at home at the Academy Theatre.

An early work assignment for me was being on the arts in high school tour team. Four of us would load up a van and go to high schools all over Georgia. I was the only African American in the group. The only things we brought with us were four black boxes. Using improvisational techniques, we would make up plays that addressed things of interest to high school students, like moving from middle school to high school or dating for the first time. The plays always had an educational bent to them. We would add music, sing, and use our bodies, our minds, and those black boxes in creative ways, climbing over one another to suggest a building or some other scene. It was hard work but I learned a lot about improvisation and live performance.

Frank Wittow founded the Academy of Theatre and Music in 1956, the year I was born. He was a godfather-like figure to many people, and I also ended up regarding him as a father figure and mentor. I loved him very much, but I wasn't as fearful of him as some others in the company were.

We used to have workshops on the weekend in which Frank would teach us more about improvisation. He taught and drilled us in many aspects of improvisation and acting: how to work off each other; how to be conscious of what you smell, feel, and taste; and how to incorporate that into a character. He taught us how to be truthful with character, and I especially enjoyed that, exploring the human body to understand what it felt like to be grounded and honest within a character. He also instructed us in ways to be flexible and to develop a variety of characters and how to make them sound and look different from one another. Frank gave me all those skills over the years I spent with him. He was a truly great teacher. I'd done a fair amount of acting and improvising when I met him, but he took me much deeper into it.

As my comfort level grew, I knew I'd be giving this a real shot. I was not going back to law school. After about a year, I was making $200 a week and it was enough to cover my rent because I lived with three other guys. I was all in, and now I believed I could have a career in the theater. But my mother took a little convincing.

"You're doing *what*? I thought you were going back to law school!"

During this time, I did a television commercial for Aaron's TV Rentals, a home furnishings rental company. I had no lines in the commercial but I remember that this woman would hit me in the stomach with her purse and say, "You could at least call your mother every now and then!" which somehow connected thematically to the idea of renting furniture. That one never ran during the Super Bowl.

At this time, my mom was working as a dietitian at a nursing home. She was watching television with one of her patients one day and the ad came on.

"That's my son!"

"Really? You can make a lot of money doing commercials."

Then they had a little chat about acting and commercials, and my mother could see there was indeed a future and a worthwhile career in acting and in the theater. She and I talked, too, and I explained some of my goals and plans to her, and she came around to the idea.

"Kenny, you have my blessing to do this. I love you and trust you. I understand it better now so just follow your heart. Do what you want to do."

For the next eight years, I was an actor and I comfortably saw myself that way. I thought that was where my gifts were. I could do it for a living and a career. The doubts of a year earlier had been dispelled by work and experience.

In those first few years, I would do these plays for high school students during the day. And at night we might do some Arthur Miller or Shakespeare. I remember playing Sir James Tyrrell in *Richard III*. We did Alice Childress's *Wedding Band: A Love/Hate Story in Black and White*, a play about interracial marriage.

By the time I arrived at the Academy Theatre in 1979, my relationship with Carol Mitchell had changed a bit, though not for any particular reason. We were embarking on our careers and adult lives. We weren't as close as we'd been in our college days, but that was simply because we hadn't seen each other as regularly. Still, working at the same place would give us a chance to reconnect, but it would all play out in an unexpected way. For the first several years, we reconnected nicely but our relationship stayed the same.

In 1985, Carol developed some health problems. She told some of her friends that she had kidney disease, which is serious, but the few details she shared about it and how to go forward were sketchy. Her way of dealing with it was to withdraw from the world. And one of the people she stopped talking to was me.

But we worked at the same place and I saw her a lot. Still, she wouldn't talk to me and flat out avoided me. As such a close friend, I was hurt and a little annoyed. What good would retreating from me, and her other friends, do?

One day, obviously angry, I confronted her outside the theater. I pressed her on why she was so distant.

"Kenny, my kidney problems are very serious," she said. "I don't think I'll be around much longer so I wanted to make things easier on the people that care about me by pulling away." I wasn't thrilled with her answer, but at least I could see her motivation.

Carol had another source of stress: she was dealing with a divorce, too.

My friend was simply having a terrible stretch in her life. She was mostly scared about her health, as anyone would be. With some clarity on her perspective, I set to work on seeing what I could do to help her.

Based on what little she would tell me, I felt that she didn't really have all the facts on what she was facing. I convinced her to go with me to the hospital to get more information on her condition from her doctors. Carol set it up, but I had to pose as her brother so I could be there with her for the visit.

As it turned out, Carol did not have a good, accurate sense of her situation. She was sick but not on death's door. It wasn't quite that bleak.

We found out that there was a path for her to take that would allow her to get healthier. If she just did a few things differently and got these particular meds, she'd be OK.

In addition to helping her understand her medical condition, I helped her move out of her home with her husband and into a new apartment. That's how I got back into her life.

During that time, we got closer and closer; closer than we had ever been before. Then that intense friendship turned into a romantic relationship. Then we ended up getting married.

At this time in my life, around 1985 to 1986, I was dating a particular kind of woman. I looked for beauty first and then I'd see if I actually liked her. After a while, these relationships gave me a certain attitude toward how men and women relate. I felt things were a bit shallow, that there was never a true depth to these connections. There was also a lack of trust in these relationships. Everybody playing games to be together. My attitude was, *Man, I can't find* that *woman because men and women just do not relate to each other in a real way. There is nothing to build on.*

When I started to get closer to Carol, previously a strictly platonic friend, and I was helping her with her medical condition, I began to think about relationships a little differently.

OK, maybe we wouldn't pick each other for each other. But maybe a relationship is about something other than body heat and attraction. Maybe it's more about being with someone that you share important things with, like intellectual curiosity and faith, books, movies, music. Maybe it's about someone who is easy to be with. Maybe I'm supposed to be dating my best friend. Carol and I trust each other, to say the least.

Around this time, Len Bias died from a cocaine overdose. He was a twenty-two-year-old basketball player at Maryland who had just been drafted by the world champion Boston Celtics. His career was just about to start and he seemed ready for stardom and success. But then he was just gone. As a sports fan, I was hit hard by his death. It was a chilling reminder that life is short and time is precious. You don't really know how much you'll get. Without being overly simplistic about it, I feel that Len Bias's story made me take a hard look at my life, and I began to feel that, maybe, my life was getting away from me. I was thirty, and I needed to get going.

When I suggested the idea of marriage to Carol, she thought I was joking. Then she was shocked.

Then she said, "Really?"

And I said, "Yes."

I didn't have a ring or get down on my knees either. It was two friends agreeing to go into unchartered waters together. We got married on May 23, 1987.

Carol's kidney disease meant she had to take very good care of herself. She was on the waiting list for a kidney transplant, and she wanted to be the best candidate she could be. She had one of those personalized dialysis machines that she used three times a day. It was a new technology that didn't work in every case but Carol was a fit. It was call CAPD, continuous ambulatory peritoneal dialysis. She ran this liquid through her body and it acted as a magnet and drew all the impurities out. This approach wasn't for everybody because it was largely self-care at home. But it suited Carol, who now wanted to take charge of her health and live her life to the fullest. She was a far cry from the woman who had begun to withdraw from the world only a few years earlier.

But she didn't want anyone to know. As a busy actress, engaged in collaborative work, it was tricky for her to conceal such a regular occurrence.

Once we got married, taking care of her and helping with her scheduling became my responsibility. I was around and could cover for her. If she and I were in a play that I was directing, I made sure that we had three breaks that would accommodate the fifteen minutes she needed each time for dialysis. In 1989, we went on vacation to Jamaica. My priority was to make sure that all of her medical supplies arrived safely ahead of us.

My role was to take care of her.

Over time, I grew quite close to Frank Wittow. So close that Carol and I actually got married in the Academy Theatre and he walked Carol down the aisle. Her father had passed away and Frank was right for the role. We made the wedding like a play. My grandmother was there, and I think it was the first time she saw me in tennis shoes in a setting where some people might find them inappropriate. I wore Reebok Alien sneakers, which were gray, red, and white high tops, with a suit from 1923 that I had worn in *Wedding Band*.

Frank was a great actor and stage director and a wonderful, effective teacher. We were a company of actors, and he oversaw our community work in the day and the legitimate shows at night. There were about twenty of us, and some of us did the high school and prison work, but we all came together at night to do whatever the main show was. It was a great experience for me and provided me with a strong foundation in my chosen field. These were good times.

I worked with a group in a prison called Emanon, which is "no name" spelled backward. It was a group of prisoners who were doing twenty-five years to life.

We went in there and did theater games with them and taught them improvisational games. We made up plays and scenes.

I quickly found out these people had no inhibitions.

I could say, "I need somebody to be an eighty-year-old woman," and this thirty-four-year-old man would utterly transform into an eighty-year-old woman. Not act like one. Become one.

I might say, "I need somebody to be an angry forty-five-year-old man who has blown his relationship with his kids," and somebody would completely become that person, including find-ing a way of portraying the void caused by missing his kids. They brought a lot of little subtleties and a lot of depth to their charac-terizations.

I think it came from being in prison and needing, wanting a release from it, even if it was just pretend. They could free them-selves and totally become another person and go to some faraway place, if only briefly. I learned there was something comforting about being somebody else.

I still tell actors of all levels of talent and accomplishment, "I've never seen a great performance that didn't have a sense of joy around it."

Even when someone is playing a bad guy. It looks like fun. It looks like they enjoy being in that skin and it seems effortless. There's no sense of making the character up. Just a sense of being the character. I encourage actors to let things happen and get to a place where they can simply explore and enjoy being someone outside themselves.

Even to this day I think back on what I learned from that experience—to get actors to stop acting.

During the time when I was working at the Academy, I also did regular work for two black theater companies, Jomandi Productions and Just Us Theatre. People still mention to me that the first time they saw me perform was with one of those black theater companies. We focused on the work of black writers, and it was a chance for me to stretch beyond the im-prov and community work and the more mainstream stuff we did on the big stage at the Academy. It says a lot about Frank that he would allow that sort of freelancing. He was serious about developing one's craft and backed up his philosophy with giving me the chance to get in that extra work and make a little money.

In his efforts to teach and develop the members of his company, Frank would let different people direct plays as part of the season. By my eighth year, I had never been asked to direct a play. I was having success as an actor so I was busy and productive, but after a while I was burning to direct a play.

Finally, I spoke up about it to Frank. Beverly Trader was a playwright and friend of mine from Atlanta and had given me her play *The Wishing Place* to read. I liked it, told Frank about it, and he let me direct it at the Academy.

It was sort of an odd play. I don't remember a lot of the specifics, but it called for leaves to fall in a living room, snow to come in through a window, and there was music involved. It was a bit out there but it allowed you to use every part of yourself and your experience. I used everything I had learned up to that point in this play. People came to see it and I thought it was a very successful production. It ran in a 100-seat theater and it was full for a few weekends. But at the end of it, Frank said at my annual review meeting, "Well, Ken, I don't think you have the skills to direct, but we do want you back as an actor."

Frank's reaction hurt on a few levels. First of all, I honestly felt that I had done a good job. Second, Frank had always told me he thought I was a great actor. His word, not mine. I was crushed that his interest in me staying on as an actor prevented him from really seeing what I did as a director. I had the feeling that he wanted me to get the directing bug out of my system because he really needed me as an actor.

After a few days, my grandmother's advice about being true to yourself came to the fore. I felt that the Academy Theatre, after eight years, was no longer the best place for me to develop. It was no longer a place I could be myself. I felt drawn to directing, but Frank made it clear he saw me only as an actor. It was obvious to me.

But I loved and respected Frank, and we were close friends. I knew I could be honest with him and preserve our friendship. I told him that I wanted to pursue directing and that I did not want to come back only as an actor. He understood and we parted amicably.

People of the Brick

One of the most memorable and important projects I worked on at the Academy of Theatre and Music was *People of the Brick*.

Frank Wittow asked his partner, Barbara Lebow, to write something that we could work on with homeless people. (I'd say Barbara was his wife because for all practical purposes she was, but they didn't believe in marriage.) I would assist Barbara as the director. Our overall goal was to gather some homeless people who were willing to tell the story of how they ended up in such dire straits. Barbara would help them with the narrative and structure, and I would help them in presenting the story on a stage.

I didn't know anything about homelessness at the time, but by the end of this endeavor, I knew firsthand how difficult and complicated that struggle can be. It was humbling. It was a chance to do what I've tried to do many times since: step into somebody's else's shoes. The bridge to connecting with people different from you is *understanding*, and you have to be willing to *try to understand*. Working on *Children of a Lesser God* taught me about the deaf community. I'll never relate to deaf people the way I did before that project. Skin color, age, gender, sexual orientation, whether you have a place to live, and whether or not you can hear—differences between people come in many different forms. And you must work to really understand people that are different from you. You don't learn a lot in your comfort zone.

We had some connections to a task force for the homeless in Atlanta, and they helped us find places where homeless people gathered. We would go to various buildings and parks and try to recruit people to join our project. We told them the specific ways that Barbara and I could help them with their stories and that they wouldn't just be standing alone and unprepared in front of an audience. The goal of the project, we explained, was to raise awareness of the homeless problem in Atlanta. We would help them help themselves by calling public attention to their plight.

At the beginning, we could not tell them that we would pay them because then we would have been overwhelmed with people wanting to do it. But for this production, money would be the wrong reason. We wanted people brave and honest enough to tell their stories for the greater good.

As the months went by, we slowly built this company of actors, homeless people who wanted the world to hear their stories. Our core group was about ten people, and they'd all had different paths to homelessness.

There was a seventy-two-year-old white woman who was a proud grandmother. But she developed some form of mental illness and lost control of her life. She disappeared from her prior life and disconnected from her friends and family. She found herself in Atlanta, a new city that she didn't know well. In a very low moment, she threw a rock through a window at City Hall and got arrested. After that was sorted out, she found herself on the street, dealing with her mental issues and having no place to live.

We had an older white man who lost his factory job in Tennessee. He came to Atlanta to find some temporary work but ended up caught in the cycle of poverty, never quite having enough money to go back to his old life.

One of the most memorable people in the group was Tracy. She told these amazing and compelling stories about surviving on the street and the challenges of trying to get off the street. She talked about how hard it was to keep her clothes fresh and trying to figure out how much blood you could give in one day or in one week. Giving blood was a way for a lot of them to make a little money.

One day, Tracy disappeared. We all sort of looked after her, and we were concerned. She was fragile and we hoped that nothing had happened to her. But we carried on without her.

The lessons for me mounted. I saw what spending a week without bathing can do to you. I learned that simply the smell of your own unwashed body can have a negative mental effect, compounding your troubles with every breath and step.

When you are homeless, how do you keep your clothes clean? I heard that some guys will bury in the ground any clothes they aren't wearing so they won't be stolen. Instead of opening a drawer for a change of clothes, these guys dig up a plastic bag they have secretly stashed underground.

We incorporated all of that and more into the play.

We learned other things along the way. Some homeless people

have difficulty with time and deadlines. You can't say, "We're going to meet on Monday at three p.m." Getting everyone together at once was hard. We would go to a likely hangout and grab a few of our actors and try to get some work done. We did this every day so eventually we began to see some progress.

Through the improvisational techniques that I had learned and developed under Frank, I was able to weave their stories together, with Barbara's help, to build the individual scenes and the whole play itself. We taught them how to do things repetitively through rehearsal so that they could repeat their performances with some consistency.

We also stressed that each performance was not specifically that actor's real story. We told them they were speaking collectively for the homeless population. We had them tell us their stories and we gathered those details, but we would mix them all up together so that each performer was telling a collective story as well as sharing parts of his or her own story. Many homeless people face similar struggles but with individual differences, such as how to solve the problem of shelter. They don't all approach it the same way. But as a group, these stories would reveal, in a personal way, the challenges of being homeless in Atlanta.

We had woven all their stories and details into a play with scenes, transitions, and music. You'd have a scene in an office setting with a homeless person trying to get a job. Then we meet and get to know a teacher who loses her job. We took all the things that we discovered about the challenges of being homeless and we integrated them into this play, interlaced them around different characters, and put the characters in one world.

After six or seven weeks of rehearsal, we felt we had something established that we could make into a show. We told our group that we planned to present the show at the Academy Theatre for two or three weeks. And that we would give the ticket revenue to them with no strings attached.

There were bumps along the way. Once we got the group going and actively participating, other people found out about it. Word spread. There was an article in the newspaper. People who had participated early and dropped out started to ask for their jobs back now that it was known that it had become a paying gig. Then Tracy returned.

She had found out that the actors in the group would be getting paid. She approached me.

"Kenny, what's going on? Somebody's takin' my spot. This is my spot. I'm in this group."

Then she pulled out a gun, a .25 caliber pistol.

I'm thinking, *Oh, shit! What the fuck, Tracy?*

She was demanding we return her to her place in the group. We gently talked her down a bit and she surrendered the gun. She calmed down rather quickly because she didn't really have that kind of anger and violence in her. We let her back in.

As we explored things with Tracy a bit deeper, we made a startling discovery.

Tracy was a man.

Honestly, all along I'd thought and accepted that Tracy was a woman. But he had developed the persona of a girl because he found that people were more caring and kind toward him if they thought he was female. He did it to protect himself.

When we got him to have that breakthrough and tell us the truth, I was stunned. He had done a great job of completely becoming a girl, to the extent of never letting his guard down with us. He had constructed a perfect disguise that none of us saw through. He had carried on a daily performance to help him survive on the streets—the ultimate acting job.

The education was ongoing. We found out that homeless people are not any more monolithic than other groups. They had landed on the streets in different ways and had different ideas about what to do about it. Some people wanted to get off the streets. Some people wanted to be on the streets. Some people were simply unable to fix the problems that had led to their homelessness, no matter how hard they tried.

It was a sobering lesson about the challenge of being homeless and how easy it was to find yourself in that position. A few things go wrong. You don't handle them quite right. And you're on the street. My Academy Theatre colleagues and I were only a paycheck away ourselves.

We presented the play, and the actors were brilliant. It was an amazing show and one of the most transformative and powerful experiences I've ever had in the theater, certainly the top one during my time at the Academy.

Working with these homeless actors never got easy. Once the run was over, we gave them each about $4,500, which was great. But now they were back in the world. Some of them came back to the theater asking, "What are we going to do now?" They were famous for a month or so. People came to see them, talk to them, and ask for their autographs. But now they were back to being homeless.

I never found out what happened to everyone after the run of the play. One woman had lost contact with her family, but because of the publicity around the play, she got back in touch. Other people found their families and friends, too. Some went back to their home states. Some people continued the life they were living when we met them. I never found out what happened to Tracy.

Along with Emanon, *People of the Brick* was an important moment in my life. I was thirty and well into a career in the theater. Due to my political science degree, my work has always been socially and politically motivated even without me consciously knowing it. That's why you're on the planet, after all. How can I effect change? To be truthful, there is an element of self-interest, too. I've learned that working with people that have something to teach me makes me a better director and a better human being.

Working with those homeless people opened my eyes a bit farther about the kind of artist I wanted to be. The bulk of my work would now have to be about reaching out and trying to understand people who are different from me. I wasn't going to solve the world's problems, but I was definitely going to try to understand my fellow men and women and to find, and shed light on, our common ground.

IV.

Be in the Room

One day in June 1988 I got a call, out of the blue, from actor, director, and producer Timothy Near. She had come to Atlanta to work for the Alliance Theatre, one of the best regional theaters in the country. She had seen *People of the Brick* and had seen me act in a play called *Split Second*, in which I played a policeman who briefly lost control and shot a person he had in handcuffs. She'd also heard about my other work as an actor and a director.

Timmy introduced herself and told me she really liked what I was doing. Then she asked if I knew about a specific grant offered by the National Endowment for the Arts and the Theatre Communications Group, a directing fellowship. I told her I wasn't fully aware of it but it sounded intriguing. Then she laid out her idea.

"I am the new associate artistic director at the Alliance Theatre. Bob Farley, from the Alaska Repertory Theatre in Fairbanks, has been hired as artistic director here at the Alliance. But he won't be here for six months. I'm running things right now. Why don't we write a proposal to the NEA/TCG for you to be our resident director for diversity for the next year?"

I don't want to be dramatic but this was, perhaps, the moment I was "discovered." Timmy Near only reached out to me because she saw my work. After eight years of working in theater, and even more of making a priority of staying true to myself, I had built up enough credits and reputation to be chosen by a seasoned theater professional for what would turn out to be a pivotal opportunity in my career.

With Timmy's help, I applied for this grant through the Alliance Theatre for me to work there for a year as a director to help integrate their theater. It was a national program, and there were only six slots. There was a committee in New York and the process was rigorous and competitive. They really got to know me and my work.

When I got the news that I had made the cut, there was a surprise involved.

The committee said to me, "We want you but we don't want you to stay in Atlanta. We don't think you need to be at the Alliance Theatre. You've shown you have the skills to direct. You did that interesting and amazing project with the homeless people. You've acted in Shakespearean plays and other types of plays, from Arthur Miller to brand-new playwrights. We see your unique and wonderful path. We think you need to know what the bigger industry looks like." I could have chosen any American city with a vibrant theater scene, like Chicago, New York, Boston, or San Francisco.

I talked to Carol and said, "Do I take this chance or do I stay in Atlanta?"

We'd been married for a little more than a year, and I was

instrumental in how she handled her health issues. But she well knew what a big break this could be.

"What do you think?" I said.

"I think you should do this," she said quickly. "This is a great opportunity. And that's what they want, so you need to leave Atlanta."

She gave me her blessing to take this next step. Given her health issues and our young marriage, it was pretty amazing of her.

Looking back, I'm not surprised. I know she would have gotten behind it eventually, but she needed no time at all. Her reaction was a perfect example of why I loved her and why we were so close, so in tune. She knew instinctively how perfect that grant program would be for me. And she didn't put herself between me and this chance to advance my career in such a meaningful way. That's the kind of woman Carol Mitchell was.

I accepted the position and just had to pick where I would go. New York was out of the question. I'd never been there, and frankly, I was afraid of it. That's *The Big City*. I knew that any real success in theater would involve Manhattan but I was not quite ready.

I picked Center Stage in Baltimore to work with artistic director Stan Wojewodski, and my time there turned out to be very important for me. It forced me to stop and look around at the world of professional theater in a deeper way. I was still a pretty young guy, and like all young people, I wanted to jump in and do my thing.

"I want to direct. Let me direct. Or let me assistant direct with you first and then I get a chance to direct."

But the people I was working with were taking a longer view. Especially Stan. I was out of my comfort zone of Atlanta. I was in Baltimore and I wanted to get right into that part of my comfort zone that I was able to bring with me, directing. Maybe they would let me direct a small workshop kind of project and then Stan would see that I could direct. Stan saw my time with his company a little differently.

"Hey, Kenny, why don't you go sit in on the board meeting today?"

I went to the meeting. It was three hours long. But I learned how a board is constructed and I learned about what their priorities were.

"Hey, Kenny, why don't you go spend some time with Peter Coleman today? Take the afternoon. And all of tomorrow."

Peter Coleman was Center Stage's managing director, the moneyman who kept the place running.

"Hey, Kenny, why don't you head over to Washington, D.C., and spend a few days with Zelda Fichandler at the Arena Stage? She basically invented regional theater in this country."

I didn't come to Baltimore to do all those things. I came to direct!

But I am glad I did them because they gave me a grounding in all that happens offstage. I didn't master those other areas immediately, but my exposure to them would come in handy as my career moved along. As they say in *Hamilton*, "Be in the room where it happens." It's such a powerful thing for young people, just to be in the presence of experts while they make decisions and do their work. So many people never get the opportunity to be in a professional setting and just be quiet and watch and learn and see how things are done. It was a really powerful lesson for me.

I see now that the NEA wanted me to expand my horizons. They felt being in another city would expose me to different artists with different ideas. I'd learned a lot in Atlanta, and it was time to move on for a bit, time to grow. They felt that there was a bit more variety in the kind of artists I'd meet in the Northeast so they were glad I'd picked Baltimore.

But the emphasis on observation was from Stan Wojewodski. He placed me in these different settings and with new people. After a few weeks of going here and there, he'd follow up with some questions or say, "Hey, let's go get a beer!" and pick my brain. And I realized I was a bit smarter than before, and maybe Stan realized that I had what it takes to be a director.

In certain situations, it's important to find out what you don't know. That's at the heart of how I approach plays. It's great to know what you know. We all must use our strengths. But I'm more interested in what I don't know.

I've used this approach in every production I've worked on since my time in Baltimore. I didn't have all the answers going into *Children of a Lesser God*. But since I went into it trying to figure out what I didn't know, my mind and my ears were open. If I had a rigid approach to casting, I would not have been open to casting Lauren Ridloff. She was working with me on learning sign language, and after a while it just struck me that she might be able to play Sarah Norman, the female lead, even though she'd never done live theater before.

But I was in observation mode, learning mode. I saw something in her because I was open to seeing something in her. I firmly believe that the answers will be given to us if we are observant and if we're listening and if we are simply living in an attentive way to receive the answers.

That powerful seed was planted in me all those years ago by Stan Wojewodski. It remains one of the most powerful and profound lessons I've learned in all my years in the theater.

I had chosen Baltimore because Stan had done a lot of interesting work with Shakespeare's plays. He had a great reputation, and quite simply, I wanted to be around someone as smart as Stan. We're quite different as directors. His aesthetic is different from mine. He would never direct the kind of plays I choose. I direct raw, kitchen sink dramas with a little edge. Stan, who is a truly great director, has a more intellectual bent to his work. Yet I learned invaluable lessons from him.

During my grant year, Timmy Near had been offered the artistic director job at the San Jose Repertory Theatre in California. She really never even settled in at the Alliance. As part of the grant work, she asked me to act in a play out there and do some community work with her. The play was *Sizwe Banzi Is Dead*, Athol Fugard's groundbreaking 1972 play about the far-reaching effects of apartheid in South Africa.

That opportunity was one of two exceptions that the NEA/TCG allowed me to pursue. I also got to direct a play at the Alliance in their small theater. It was called *T Bone N Weasel*, and it starred Bill Nunn.

One day, Stan said, "Kenny, can you come up with a plan for a project for yourself?"

I'd been expecting this offer for a while, and I'd given it a lot of thought. Still, I was making this up as I went along, and I really didn't know what I was doing. But that was fine. The purpose of the fellowship was to learn and grow. Stan had shown me that.

"I'd like to take some board members and some people from our community to New York to see a play by this new black writer," I said. "After the show, I'll talk to them about my experience of growing up black and apply that to the play."

Fences, by August Wilson.

Stan loved the idea and we booked the trip.

It's 1987. I'm thirty-one years old and have been working in the world of the dramatic arts for most of the previous fifteen years. But I've never felt so connected to a piece of theater.

As I sat there in the 46th Street Theatre (now the Richard Rodgers Theatre), my first time in a Broadway theater, I was deeply affected. As I watched the story of the Maxson family unfold, I could feel my grandmother's energy and rhythms. I could smell her kitchen. I felt a connection to my own family, heritage, and background. The link between my life and August's characters was very clear and very real. That night, theater became much more to me than it had ever been.

Worthy of Being on a Raised Stage

That legendary production of *Fences* featured wonderful and accomplished actors such as James Earl Jones, Mary Alice, and Courtney B. Vance. But the stars were August Wilson's words and the world he created. It was vibrant and alive, a world I knew and recognized.

Broadway is the pinnacle of the theater world. As I sat there, I could feel the history and the presence of all the artists who had presented their stories, at the highest level, in rooms just like that one. There were culturally significant showcases for these stories and storytellers.

At the same time, I was acutely aware that there are not many examples of dramatic African American storytelling. I knew that our culture and our stories had been left out.

It was nearly an out-of-body experience for me to sit there as a black American in an audience of mostly white Americans and have us all hear an authentic story from my part of America.

Not a sanitized, removed portrayal of black life.

Not a show in which black people are minor, one-dimensional side characters.

Not *Uncle Tom's Cabin* or *Gone with the Wind*.

But August Wilson's *Fences*.

For the whole show, I saw a life I knew and had in my own way lived, represented on that stage. So many lines struck me, like a hug from Grandma Mamie or a call from my mother.

"Don't you try and go through life worrying about if somebody like you or not. You best be making sure they doing right by you."

That's the way we talk.

I also felt a sense of pride because the broader community was hearing and seeing this raw, authentic, and real portrayal of black life in America as rendered by a black playwright.

August liked to put it this way:

Our stories are worthy of being on a raised stage.

That evening was a turning point in my life. It suddenly became clear to me as I looked at the set and listened to the actors.

We belong up there, too.

And for the first time as I watched a play, hearing the distinct pattern and rhythm of black speech as I had spoken it and heard it all my life, it was not theater anymore.

My life had run straight into what I do. That night gave me a sense of purpose and understanding about what this theater game could accomplish.

This feeling is why I didn't finish law school.

This feeling is why I don't lead a church.

This feeling is why I am not a politician.

Creating this feeling in others is what I should do.

Creating this feeling in others will be my ministry.

This is what Grandma Mamie wanted me to find. And do.

This is what my mother meant when she told me I was going to be someone who can effect change.

Seeing *Fences* that night delivered all those messages to me. But one guiding insight crystallized it all.

I can use our stories.

Everything that I have experienced and come to know in my life can be recontextualized and presented to an audience. I can look close to home for stories to tell and issues to raise.

As I sat there, I put more value on my grandmother's life.

I put more value on my mother's life.

I put more value on my own life.

I put more value on my voice and vowed to work harder to find that voice.

August Wilson helped me see all of that. If his mother's words are worthy, my mother's words are worthy. If his grandmother's words are worthy...

I saw my uncles on that stage.

Through August, I hear and feel my grandmother—the way she speaks, the work her generation did, the journey that they took to get to where we are today.

I am an extension of an August Wilson play. That's who I am. If he was writing another play now, I would be in it.

August wrote specifically about Pittsburgh, but the universal is discovered through the specific. And he was so deliberate in the details.

The way the people talk.

In *The Piano Lesson*, Berniece is doing Maretha's hair on a Sunday morning. In the middle of a scene, Berniece is straightening

Maretha's hair and she's talking, distracted, and burns the back of her daughter's neck. Maretha says, "Ow!" And I felt it.

I flash back because I know exactly what that is. They use Royal Crown hair dressing (we called it "grease"). And my mother burned my arm with a straightening comb while doing some-body's hair in our kitchen. I've seen so much of my own life onstage in August's plays.

August refers to the blues they sang and how they buried their people.

He wrote about superstitions.

And his characters discuss their concerns about what it takes to be American.

All those things...that's me. That's me in the most real way. It's like holding a mirror up to my life. The closest I've come to really looking myself in the mirror artistically is through his work.

As I watched that play, I could actually see and feel my earlier life unfold again in a rush created by this stunning new perspective.

I would never be the same.

When I went out to San Jose to spend that time with Timmy Near and act in *Sizwe Bansi Is Dead*, August was out in California working on a regional production of *Joe Turner's Come and Gone*, his next play, which had not been published yet. We met very briefly out there, and I do remember one thing he told me.

"Look, Kenny. Whenever you want to do one of my shows, even if they're running on Broadway, you can do my shows." It was an offer I had no intention of refusing.

I always respected that remarkable gesture from August. It is rare for any writer to feel that empowered, to disregard the proper commercial trajectory of a play. The usual course is to carefully guide a play to Broadway and not let it be diminished by other productions happening at the same time. Keep the focus on the big show, on Broadway. But August was always his own man. They were his plays and he made an exception with me, another one of Grandma Mamie's prayers coming true for me.

At the end of the NEA fellowship, the Alliance Theatre had an offer for me. They had not replaced Timmy as associate artistic director. They wanted me to take the job.

One very productive year after quitting the Academy Theatre, I was now the associate artistic director at the Alliance Theatre. It's a $15 million theater, and I'm second in command. I know that I left the Academy Theatre at the right time and for the right reasons. I had to listen to my heart and move on when it stopped feeling right. But I could not have foreseen things would work out this well. The lessons of Grandma Mamie and my mother were becoming more and more ingrained in me as I moved along in my career. Believing in myself, that I had what it took to succeed and advance in my field, was paying off.

The Alliance had been preparing for me to direct a Lorraine Hansberry play, *Les Blancs*. Hansberry died with the play incomplete, and her husband, Robert Nemiroff, finished it.

I read it and felt like it still needed some work. I called Nemiroff because he was the executor of his wife's estate and asked if he would be willing to keep playing around with it. He was firm in his refusal.

The next play I would direct was a big moment in my life as I started my career at the Alliance. It had to be right. So I told my colleagues that I didn't feel *Les Blancs* was ready and I did not want to direct it.

"What play do you want to direct?"

"I've met this writer, August Wilson," I said. "He's written this new play, *Joe Turner's Come and Gone*, which is not even published yet. I saw it out in San Jose and I love it."

I called him and asked if I could direct *Joe Turner* at the Alliance in Atlanta, and he said, "Absolutely." As promised.

So the first play I directed as associate artistic director of the Alliance Theatre was *Joe Turner's Come and Gone* by August Wilson. It was significant for several reasons. I was delivering on my directive to broaden the range of plays at the theater. And I had snagged the latest play from the hottest new playwright in the country.

Joe Turner was a big hit, and it showed everybody that I was up to the task. It was also the first play that I worked closely with August on. I asked him to come down during previews and give me notes. Going forward, whenever August had a new play, I would direct it in Atlanta and he would consult personally with me each time.

I started as associate artistic director in 1988.

By 1990, change was afoot at the Alliance Theatre.

For those two years, I worked well with Bob Farley, the artistic director. We were close and talked all the time. We had a good relationship despite being quite different.

He was quiet; I was loud. He didn't like doing large-cast plays while I enjoyed that kind of a challenge. He was a bit of an introvert with the board, but I found myself being able to communicate very well with them.

For many reasons, word got out that the Alliance was going to replace Bob as artistic director. Bob and his wife put up a bit of a fight for him to keep his position. For a short time, frankly, we all fought against that decision. We'd been doing well under Bob's leadership. I always appreciated that one of the points Bob made in his favor was that he had brought in Kenny Leon. But they had their ideas about what Bob was not good at or was not delivering.

I was separate from the whole process, but I would have done anything asked of me to help keep Bob at the Alliance. However, the decision was not happening with my input or involvement of any kind. They had decided not to renew his contract and they were moving on. The company would be conducting a national search.

When they started the search, I was just wondering who my new boss would be. But once we all understood what they were doing and there was no use in opposing it, a member of the search committee sat me down for a conversation.

"Kenny, we like what we've seen from you over the last several years," he said. "Would you throw your hat into the ring for this artistic director job?"

"Sure. I can do some important things well. I'm good with people. I can cast and direct plays. I can find good plays and playwrights. But the administrative end of things is where I'll need help and time to learn and grow."

"Fine. We'll take that into consideration."

I was both surprised and energized by the offer to become a candidate for the job. I was confident that with time I could learn to do all that the job entailed. But I'd been associate artistic director for only two years and wasn't entirely sure enough people would think I'd had sufficient seasoning and experience to handle the top job.

One of the people who supported my candidacy was a special man named Jennings Hertz, an Atlanta businessman and devoted patron of the arts. A board member at the Alliance, Jennings felt that I was the one to lead the theater into a new era of integration and expansion. They wanted to retain their current audience, but they also wanted to create new theatergoers and they wanted to do that by demonstrating a willingness to reach out to the community actively and to be willing to stretch the repertoire of the theater to include a more diverse palette of plays and playwrights. *Death of a Salesman* followed by *"Master Harold"... and the Boys*. The work of Arthur Miller, Athol Fugard, August Wilson, and Wendy Wasserstein would all be welcome at the Alliance.

Jennings brought in Lloyd Richards to address the board on my behalf. After vouching for me artistically and declaring me up to the task, Lloyd also offered a piece of advice for them.

"If you hire Kenny Leon, and I hope you do, hire him because you think he's the best candidate. And remember that when times get tough."

I got the job as artistic director of the biggest regional theater in the South. Just a few short years after working with prisoners and inmates. I couldn't help but notice that it was possible because of my own personal Holy Trinity: Grandma Mamie, my mother, and August Wilson. My family helped me with their lifelong support and belief in me. And August helped me with his transformative work and his willingness to let me present that work.

A Place to Hear Everybody's Story

When I started as artistic director at the Alliance Theatre, as noted by the search committee, I probably knew about 50 percent of the job.

But I knew what I could do well. I knew I could direct plays, and I knew that I liked reaching out to the community. Early on, I planned a lot of events, such as the Lunchtime with Kenny series, which helped us engage with the local population and let them in on our plans.

Over time, I would learn about budgeting and managing people and the other vital aspects of running such a big organization.

My contract also required me to go away at least once a year to direct a play in another part of the country. I would eventually direct plays in Boston, Chicago, and Hartford. This practice allowed me to grow as a director, meet new actors and theater people from across the country, and evolve professionally by seeing how other major theaters operate. These sabbaticals of mine also spread the word about the Atlanta theater scene and the Alliance Theatre in particular.

At the time I took over, there was a priority that I would need to address, one I supported strongly. The Alliance Theatre wanted to develop and reinforce a specific mission.

Jennings Hertz said it best: "We have to strive for excellence in our pursuit of telling everybody's story."

When I came to the Alliance Theatre, it was more than 90 percent white and more than 90 percent people who could easily afford theater tickets. It definitely wasn't a place to go to hear everybody's story.

As I got settled in, I realized that I would have to make it clear what my mission was, what the mission of the theater as an entity was. I knew there would be resistance. Many people go to the theater to escape. We'd have to walk a fine line if we were to achieve our goals. I'd need to put together seasons that reflected classic entertainments that people knew and were comfortable with and other more challenging works that used different voices and perspectives. It was hard but I never forgot how important it was.

When I was first named artistic director, I got some beautiful letters of support, from all kinds of people. It was a great feeling.

I also received this one:

When we come to the theater, we come to support our own kind. Not some pushy, uppity coon.

It concluded with a death threat.

Carol and I were a bit nervous at first. But then we both quickly came up with the same reaction.

"This is just weakness, cowardice. A weak person hiding behind a letter."

"Right. And all we're doing is running a theater," said Carol. "You're not Dr. King. Can you imagine what his life was like?"

We laughed it off together. This was before social media so the impact was less striking. Still, it reminded me that our plans for the theater would meet resistance.

We focused on the positive and the support. At that time, there was nothing I would do that I wouldn't talk to Sam Jackson about. He was kind of the reason I was doing theater. When I told him about the offer, he said, "Oh, my brother! Go and kill it, man! You can do it!" And when I told him about the hateful letter, he said, "Fuck that. Go run your theater. Many more people want you in that job than don't. Do your thing."

The support was pretty overwhelming. It was all "Atlanta's own Kenny Leon. We loved him at the Academy Theatre. We're so happy he'll be at the Alliance."

I heard from white, black, Christian, and Jewish people, and they were all excited about what lay ahead for me and the Alliance Theatre.

The challenges were there to be addressed so I focused on my strengths at first. Thanks to Stan Wojewodski, I knew to think about the whole operation, not just the main stage. That training paid off immediately.

But I always knew how to engage people. When I was the associate director at the Alliance, I started an initiative called Lunchtime with Kenny. I would invite writers, actors, and the other creative people involved with a play we were presenting to come and talk to the community before we presented the play. It was a way to create interest in the play and also a chance to spread our philosophy to our audience in a way that would pay off down the road, too. I had a bit of a following with these lunches, and my first several shows were very well received. We were off to a good start in what we were trying to build. Now as artistic director, I continued that community outreach and gospel spreading.

For the first three or four years, we were on a high. There were 20,000 subscribers when I started as artistic director. There was the hoped-for influx of new people, too. We were able to integrate the theater because I was all about diversity, rewriting the mission statement to focus on inclusion and the dialogue about race in our country. I introduced new playwrights such as Pearl Cleage, the Atlanta-based writer of *Blues for an Alabama Sky*, which I directed at the Alliance with Phylicia Rashad and Bill Nunn. We developed a great relationship with Pearl, and I told her if she wrote a play, we'd produce it. Atlanta's Alfred Uhry, who wrote the play and movie of *Driving Miss Daisy*, also worked with us at the Alliance. I directed his play *The Last Night of Ballyhoo*, which premiered at the Alliance during the 1996 Olympics and won the 1997 Tony Award for best play in 1997. These plays and others that addressed issues of race and identity helped to integrate the theater and brought us a new audience.

In 1993, our work at the Alliance had begun to receive national notice and attention. The Reader's Digest Foundation gave us a grant of $3 million specifically because we were taking on issues of race consistently. They wanted to support those efforts, and $3 million is a game-changing contribution to a regional theater. Things were looking good.

But about five years in, we also sensed a bit of pushback from longtime subscribers. Subscribers were down to 17,000 to 18,000 from the peak of 20,000, but those were still very respectable numbers. White middle-class theatergoers were expressing the idea that I was doing too many African American stories. We usually did eleven plays in a season, and if three of them were African American or contained a racial or an ethnic theme, then some people felt that was too many. Other people felt I was trying to force something down their throats. Looking back, I can say that I might have focused too much on bringing new people down to the Woodruff Arts Center, where the Alliance was based. I could have spent more time nurturing our existing audience and supporters.

By 1997, our subscriptions were down to about 14,000. This period was quite challenging because there was clear pushback from people who didn't value our emphasis on diversity. Some people just didn't embrace the changes at the Alliance. They wanted what they wanted, which was the traditional slate of familiar plays and musicals, with the occasional new show. But not three or four plays per season that were not light evenings out. I felt these people misunderstood me and what we were trying to do. Their stories and points of view were important to me. I was just trying to give voice on a regular basis to perspectives that were not commonly heard, as August Wilson said, on a raised stage.

At the same time, we had made a lot of progress. I had a huge fan base that understood what we were doing. This is what change looks like. There will be bumps along the road but the journey remains worth it. Still, the board had a decision to make.

We were losing subscribers, which is a significant issue. But other parts of the company's overall goals were in hand. We were gaining a national reputation. Work done under my watch had led to an increase in media coverage and recognition. Generally speaking, our focus on diversity was well received and praised. People were excited by the works of Pearl Cleage, Alfred Uhry, and August Wilson. We'd done a very successful collaboration with Disney on *Aida*. We'd received that grant from Reader's Digest.

My friend and board member Jennings Hertz summed it up beautifully in a meeting with the board.

"Remember what Lloyd Richards said when we were doing the search that led us to select Kenny? He said to remember the choice we made when times get tough. Those times are here. Are we going to still love Kenny Leon?"

The board decided that they did. They felt that the good of my tenure outweighed the loss of some subscribers. They wanted a national theater. They wanted black, white, Jewish, and Latino people sitting next to one another in our theater. We might lose some people, but we'd get by. They stuck with me. We never got the numbers up near 18,000 to 20,000 again, but nobody did. The recession hit and regional theaters took some losses just like every other business.

I was relieved, of course, and grateful for the support. In doing work that confronts issues and provokes people, you have to be ready for the part of the audience that simply does not want that. But our board proved themselves to be consistent and brave. They stayed true to the mission and accepted the subscriber losses as a reasonable cost of doing business the way we wanted.

Money often talks the loudest in these situations. But the board wasn't listening this time.

Independence and a Parting

In 1990, I was in a pretty good place. I was running the major theater company in Atlanta, and my wife was the top actress in town. No one made any charges of nepotism because, frankly, everyone wanted to work with her. I'd have been a fool not to have Carol work with us at the Alliance.

Christmas Day in 1991 brought the most amazing gift, but one that would change everything.

That day, the hospital called to say there was a kidney available for Carol. And after she received the kidney, her life changed. And so did mine.

She reclaimed her independence and, to be honest, didn't really need me to navigate her medical issues and the accommodations that went along with them. But, as we soon discovered, my playing that role was instrumental in maintaining the closeness of our relationship, our marriage.

Her attitude, however subtle and below the surface, was:

OK. Now I'm back to myself. I don't need all this help.

What this transformation showed was that, in the end, we

were the greatest of friends. And we probably should have just remained friends.

Make no mistake. The day she got her kidney transplant was beautiful. Soon after, we turned in that CAPD and celebrated. But as time passed, it became evident that we had different interests and some distance set in between us. Her health had bound us together in a loving way, but her health had dramatically improved. Those bonds loosened.

Before we got married, I'm pretty sure she felt that she wasn't my type. And her attitude was, *That's my brother.* That's the way it always was in her head.

But once we got together, she likely romanticized it all a little bit.

Here we are, the top two actors in Atlanta. And now Kenny's become a director, and he's running the big theater company. We're supposed to be together.

She also knew I had her back. She knew she could count on me. And while I'm no saint, our first five years of marriage had pretty much backed that idea up. I was there for her. But after she got her kidney, months went by and I started to feel a change. It seemed to me we now wanted different things.

Before we got married, I should have asked Carol some very important questions. I should have found out her attitude toward family, religion, romance, and other meaningful things. We assumed we knew each other well enough when her medical condition drew us closer. But when her health improved, we lost that reason to be so close. I didn't need to take care of her anymore, and that changed everything.

After the next four or five years, things really fell apart but we didn't divorce. By year seven or eight, I was looking around at other possibilities in life, but I didn't want to do the wrong thing either.

As usually happens, things got tough when we had to break apart. I didn't like doing it, but I also knew it was long overdue. I walked down the stairs with a television under my arm. I gave her the house and everything else.

On one level, she understood it. But when I actually left and the divorce was final in 1998, some anger set in on her part. When we first got divorced, we went through a period in which she didn't want to have much to do with me.

After our divorce, Carol continued to act but her love was teaching. She taught acting at Clark Atlanta University for twenty years, placing teaching the craft over her own career. She once told me, "I'm supposed to teach these students at Clark. If I get to act in a play or make a movie now and then, that's my dessert." She had a small role in *Fried Green Tomatoes* and Hollywood definitely called, but she went with her heart. She was true to herself and had no regrets about her career.

Time passed, and we saw or heard very little of each other. It was for the best. But in November 2006, I got a call from Carol's dear friend Debbie Barber, who was Carol's health-care guardian and the executor of her estate. Carol's kidney had begun to fail and she was in a serious state. Carol was in the hospital and wanted me to visit. Maybe for one last time.

I arrived at the hospital the week of Thanksgiving, and I must say that I wish we all could have a Debbie Barber in our lives.

She was so caring and protective of Carol, who had lapsed into a coma.

As we stood in Carol's room, Debbie gave me the rest of the story.

"Kenny, they want to undo all the machines," she said through tears. "They want to pull everything, but I just can't do it. They're saying, basically, she's brain-dead, but I know she's still here. I know what they mean and I have to do something. But I don't want to do it now because I don't want to remember Carol this way every year at Thanksgiving."

I said, "OK. Step out of the room and let me handle this."

Now I'm alone with Carol and I start talking to her.

"Yo, Carol. I know we've been through some shit. But one thing we do know is that we love each other."

Her eyes are closed and she's still. The only sound in the room is the hiss and whirr of the machines keeping her alive.

"Look. All I know is if you want to fight for your life, then you need to do it now. They're getting ready to shut these machines down. Let's have this be your decision. If you're ready to go, then release. But if you're not, you have to show a sign. You have to let them know that you're not ready to go."

And then I left.

The next morning, I get a call from Debbie.

"Kenny, you will not believe this. The nurse just called me. She said when she came into the room, Carol opened her eyes and said, 'Happy Thanksgiving!'"

Carol lived a little over two more years, passing away in January 2009. She stayed in that hospital for a bit longer and then moved to a rehabilitation center in Florida. She had to rebuild her strength and learn to walk again. I visited her there a few times and also visited her when Debbie brought her back to Atlanta near the end of her life, and I saw her just before she passed.

Carol was about 80 percent of herself those last years. She'd been through so much.

I was surprised to get that call about her coming out of the coma because I really thought she was slipping away. After that call, I thought, *Well, she must have heard me! She did what I said. She told them, "I ain't ready to go!"* But that was Carol. Nobody told her where or when to go.

That story about Carol taught me about the spiritual life and how we're here until we're not here. I know she heard what I said, and I was glad for the chance to help her and let her have those last years.

We never really talked about that episode seriously. I would joke about it.

"You know, you was like outta here!"

And she would laugh. But she was not the same old Carol. She was bedridden and we didn't talk very deeply anymore. It's not like we suddenly became best friends again.

She loved me and I loved her. She was glad for those visits and was always happy to see me. Our friendship had taken so many turns so it was nice that it ended in a gentle, loving way.

I don't have any regrets about my story with Carol Mitchell, except for any pain I may have caused her. The best part of our relationship was the glue that made us the best friend either one of us ever had. I don't know if she would have had the strength to take on those health issues if I wasn't around. And she was a great source of stability in my life as I began my time at the Alliance Theatre, which was a big job that brought stress and uncertainty, as well as great opportunity, to my career. We were supposed to be together at that time to help each other navigate that time in our lives. The parting was difficult, but it didn't lessen the importance and the value of the time we had together.

There Is No Picture of
Perman Wilson

Grandma Mamie shared her love and wisdom with me easily for as long as I was blessed to know her. One of her favorite sayings was:

You're not old until you can't do for yourself!

And Grandma was a woman who could take care of herself. She lived alone the last half of her life, driving her own car until she was eighty-five, doing her own shopping and cooking her own food. After a less than perfect marriage and raising thirteen children, I always felt that Grandma prized her independence. She was never a selfish person. Still, I am glad that she got to spend her later years in good health and doing the things that brought her happiness and peace. Just thinking of her washes those feelings over me.

Time catches everyone, though. In 1991, Grandma was visiting with my mom and other family one day and she was really struggling with knee pain. Grandma Mamie was physically very strong, and a lot of that strength came from her legs, even though they were noticeably bowed. In her mid-eighties, her knees had given out and they needed to be replaced. The family convinced her to go up north, stay with family, and get the necessary surgery.

Most people would have one procedure, recover from it, and then have the other one. But Grandma Mamie was not most people. She did what she wanted.

"If I'm gonna do it, I'm gonna do them both at the same time."

And that's what she did, but it proved to be her downfall. She was eighty-seven, and both her knees were in need of rest and rehabilitation. Not being able to move very well at all really slowed her down and brought on other serious complications.

After she was well enough to travel back home, Grandma began to decline. She was still proud and tried to assert her independence but her body wasn't up to it anymore. She went into the hospital for various things. And one day I got a call from my mother.

"Kenny, you need to get here."

We have a very big family, and Tony and I were the last ones to get to her bedside. I took her hand and she knew I was there.

"Oh, Kenny. I'm so ready."

Of course, I felt sad. I knew what she meant. But I also felt, yet again, astonishment and wonder at how this woman conducted her life, and now her death. She lay there in peace and contentment. She was tired and had led a long and wonderful life. She embraced the next chapter with such ease. I remember thinking that I wanted to have that kind of faith, strength, and preparedness. She was ready to go, and she was calm and she gently squeezed my hand.

She passed two days later.

When I got the word, I was in Minnesota at a conference, flew home, and drove to Florida with Carol. I didn't cry when I found out. Probably because my last visit with her was so gentle and sweet. I knew she hadn't been in great pain. She was eighty-seven, and it wasn't unexpected.

As I drove, Carol slept, and I was alone with my thoughts. They took me back to that porch on Miccosukee Road, a little boy and his grandmother, talking and laughing and playing "That's your car!"

At her funeral, the preacher took me out back behind the church to the nicely kept graveyard and to the river where we all were baptized.

"Your grandmother is responsible for this graveyard."

"Responsible for it?"

"Over thirty years ago, Mamie used to say that we needed to have a cemetery fund to clean up the plots after they had fallen into disrepair. The church council voted on it and it lost. Every Sunday after that, she would put a dollar in an envelope and write "Cemetery Fund" on it. Some others did, too, but it was your grandmother's idea. After a while, we had enough money to clean it all up and maintain it as she thought we should. She was a great woman."

I never knew the story about the cemetery fund until that day. But that was Grandma Mamie. You don't have to wait on the world. When you believe in something, you just do it.

It might sound like an exaggeration but Grandma Mamie is part of my everyday existence. The world is full of things that remind me of her or of things she used to say. One of her favorite expressions was:

Everybody on the bed or everybody on the floor.

Grandma Mamie would say that if ten or more people would visit her. She had one extra bed so everybody couldn't fit. But she prized fairness. Decide whatever you want but everyone is treated the same way. There won't be two in the bed and eight on the floor. Not in Mamie's house.

When I'm doing a play, I am building an ensemble. Everyone is responsible for the production. The famous people have to do all the stuff that everybody else does. When someone is late for rehearsal, I penalize everyone.

"OK. John is late. Ten push-ups for everyone." And that includes me. I hit the floor myself.

We're building a team, and we're also acknowledging that if someone's late, it holds things up; it affects us all. I share Grandma Mamie's sense of fairness with everyone I work with, usually in the first talk I give once the team is together.

Everybody on the bed or everybody on the floor.

Over the years, I have found that people who are close to us and mean the most are seen more clearly and sharply in our minds. We see their clothes more vividly; we remember more details. And people who have just come into our lives or are not that important to us are more faded and fuzzy in our minds and memories.

Family pictures help with our efforts to keep departed people close. You look through a family album and see an old familiar face, and the picture in your mind brightens and becomes more alive.

There is no picture to be found of Mamie's husband, Perman

Wilson, my grandfather. He had thirteen children but no one has a photo of him. My mother loved her father, but she tells me he's fading in her mind.

"I'm trying to hold on to him," she says. "But as time goes on, I've mostly lost the image."

That will never happen with me and Grandma Mamie. I think of her every day, and she pops up in different scenes. Always bright and crisp and clear.

I see her getting ready for church in those colorful hats.

I see her on the porch, reading the paper and talking with me.

I see her in the kitchen preparing food.

I see her in her seat watching *Fences* by August Wilson.

I see her smiling at me, and my heart fills.

I see my grandma Mamie.

I always will.

Aida

Just as my grandmother adjusted to changes in the world around her, I have had to do the same in my work in the theater. When Disney came to me with a potential project, I had a balancing act to perform, and as usual, the lessons of Grandma Mamie came in handy. This story is a great example of how staying true to yourself, your vision, and your promises can produce a successful and, in this case, unexpected result.

I also learned the wisdom of "Ask and you shall receive."

By 1998, I had been working at the Alliance Theatre in Atlanta for ten years. We were trying to diversify the programming as well as the audience, trying to lead our subscribers to an understanding of our message of integration and inclusion. A big part of that was introducing African American writers and doing plays that ask questions of the audience. It was going well but we weren't finished.

Back then, we produced six plays on the main stage and four plays in the studio or children's theater. I chose each season's productions, and assigned creative teams to each play, with great care. It was a difficult but important part of my job because I was very interested in what those plays said to our community.

Founded in 1993, Disney Theatrical Productions had done very well with live productions of *Beauty and the Beast* and *The Lion King* when they came to me with a proposal. Disney had been working for about two years on an adaptation of Giuseppe Verdi's *Aida* with music by Elton John and lyrics by Tim Rice. The show was definitely headed to Broadway, but it needed a try-out at a regional theater. I'm sure there were many reasons that they reached out to us at the Alliance Theatre, but I bet it didn't hurt that Elton John has a home in Atlanta.

When Disney first got in touch to discuss having a partnership in the development of this show, I was flattered but declined the offer. At that time, I was well into delivering on the mission we had at the Alliance Theatre. Our shows were about the continuation of the discussion of race. That ongoing dialogue was important for our shows. We sought to entertain, of course, but the plays have to be driven a certain way. I wasn't sure *Aida* was for us. Now was not the time to send a possibly confusing message to our board and our 15,000 subscribers, a message that could be interpreted as our placing more emphasis on the commercial aspects of live theater.

A few months later, Disney got back in touch and asked me to elaborate on my reservations. After all, I wasn't sure about it but I had fears just the same. I had a phone call with Tom Schumacher and Peter Schneider of DTP and they said, "What are you afraid of?"

I briefly explained my position to them on the phone and they said, "Well, write down the specific things you have concerns about and we will look at each one with you."

After writing about the mission concerns et al., I delved a bit into other possible conflicts I saw.

I told them that the premise of the show was perfect for our theater. A black woman and a white man torn from their cultures because they love each other. They choose to die together rather than live apart because their love is so strong. That's what we do at the Alliance Theatre.

But there was already a director in place. There was a full creative team in place as well. I was concerned that they would put me and my team on the sideline in our own theater.

Schumacher put me at ease quickly. He said, "No. We want you to have creative input, and we will respect your creative input. This is your institution, and if we ever come to a fork in the road over anything, we will defer to your judgment." And then they did even more to put me at ease.

At my request, the Disney people helped me deliver assurances to all interested parties that this production was not counter to what we were building at the Alliance Theatre. Disney CEO Michael Eisner hosted a gathering for some of our board members so they felt special and included. Schumacher addressed some staff and members of the community at a breakfast meeting.

Very quickly, through words and actions, they dispelled all of my initial fears. Most important, as it turned out, was their willingness, despite already having their own director and creative team for the production, to make me an active creative participant. They would also be using some of our production staff to build the sets and work with costumes and lighting and all that goes into mounting a show like *Aida*. They made it feel like a true partnership so I agreed to place the show onto our schedule.

I was also not unaware of the economic implications of teaming up with a corporate partner like Disney. If this show proved successful, the Alliance Theatre company would see some financial rewards long after the show left town. We, of course, got a piece of the ticket sales in Atlanta, but we also would get a weekly check when it ran on Broadway. My challenge was to secure that monetary benefit without selling out our vision by standing aside and just letting them take over our theater for a few months. If I had not stuck to my guns with Disney about our theater's values, I would have betrayed years of my own statements about our goals and vision. It would have been hard to go back to building the audience as we had been.

DTP had been working and developing the show since about 1996. One of the distinctive aspects of the production when it arrived in Atlanta was the centerpiece of the set, a big pyramid that could change shape to suggest different locations like a ship or the inside of a palace. The director, Robert Jess Roth, had directed *Beauty and the Beast* on Broadway for Disney after having worked on live shows at Disney theme parks. The pyramid was a radical idea, combining a theme park ride, in a way, with something appropriate for a live theater production. This technology had never been tried before.

The pyramid weighed five tons. You had to be careful around it. We could never get it to work consistently because it kept leaking hydraulic fluid along with other mechanical problems. They couldn't quite solve the science of it. But when it worked, it was beautiful.

One night during previews for the show, we were very close to curtain and the pyramid would not work. I quickly huddled with my Disney partners and they had what they felt was the obvious solution. Cancel the show, refund the money, and work hard to fix it for tomorrow. They wanted to handle it like a New York commercial production. The show can't go on and this is how you solve that.

But I saw it differently, and here was a chance for me to assert the power they had given me.

"OK, guys, I see your point," I said. "But I am the creative director here. My thought is that community theater is different from Broadway commercial theater. People have marked tonight on their calendars. They have gotten dressed up and they hired babysitters. Plus, I think people like it when things sort of don't work perfectly. It's part of the excitement of live theater."

They were a bit surprised but listening to me.

"Here is my plan," I continued. "I'll go in front of my subscribers and I'll explain the situation. Then I want all the actors and singers to come onstage, sit down in some chairs, and we do the whole play. It will be different but the audience will definitely feel like they are in this house on a special night."

They agreed. They had to. We had decided that I would make the call in a moment like that.

I went onstage, cleared my throat, and said, "Hello, everybody. We're glad you're here. As you know, we are in previews for *Aida*. We are working with Disney as a partner, and I promise you that this is a great production. We are thrilled to be participating. But this is live theater and the technology is not working with us tonight. I'm going to ask you to go with us right now. The show must go on. The actors will give you everything they got. I just ask you to be with us."

We did it, and it was beautiful. It was a great night for me because, in that setting, I saw how amazing the show was. The Disney team, my theater group, and the actors had done such incredible work. And Elton John and Tim Rice are astounding artists. Their work was so strong that it carried that unusual presentation without any lessening of impact or entertainment. That was one of the major takeaways, not to let the technology overshadow the story and the music.

We did fix the pyramid and continued to use it during the two-month run. Most of the time it worked, but some nights it didn't. When it didn't, we did the show as on that preview night, including my pre-show explanation. When the show left Atlanta for a run in Chicago, the decision was made to come up with a way to do the show without the pyramid. That one night had shown them they didn't need it. And it ran on Broadway for four and a half years without that pyramid.

Aida and Disney got all they could have wanted out of their run at the Alliance Theatre in Atlanta. I wasn't day to day on the project when it left our town but they respected my input, especially as an African American artistic director.

I learned a lot working on *Aida*. If you have good, well-intentioned people on the corporate side, you can form great partnerships. Disney had become a major player in live theatrical productions, but they demonstrated a great respect for what I and the Alliance Theatre team could do for their production of this new and important show. They invited us to join them, and it really worked out. And their trust in me and my team led them to uncover a very important piece of information: their show did not need the $10 million, five-ton pyramid. That alone made the Atlanta run invaluable to them.

After that experience, I've had a healthy respect for corporate involvement. It can help immensely if you know how to handle things. As it turned out, Disney and I were coming from the same place. And they weren't too big to see it. We listened to each other, and it was all for the good of the show. That's how you do it.

My conviction and my strength in dealing with Disney were direct gifts from my grandma more than anybody:

You gotta be you. If you're not you, you're gonna regret it.

In many situations, it's natural to feel fear. Am I making the wrong decision here? Still, no matter the result, you'll feel worse if you don't listen to that voice you're hearing deep down.

I've always been very comfortable being me and living my life. That approach has always felt better even when I didn't win. Sometimes you see people in our industry make decisions based solely on one value, which is usually financial. If you do that, and betray those other parts of you, even though you're making a million dollars, you know you betrayed yourself. Your success will have an uneasy quality to it. It won't sit right and you'll feel it.

Everything about *Aida* in Atlanta sat right. And everyone involved benefited.

Around this time, some special people entered my life. We did an integrated, multiracial production of *A Christmas Carol*, written by David Bell, my associate artistic director at the Alliance. Seven-year-old Maria Thompson came in for an audition. She was beautiful and talented, and her audition went very well. I cast her in the play.

Because she was so young, I asked her, "Where's your mom?" Maria pointed out her mom to me. Jennifer Thompson had on this stunning pink dress, and I can still recall her walking down a long hallway at the theater in that dress. She was married at the time, and we didn't see each other that much. But I'd met her daughter. And seen that dress.

Soon after, Maria came to me in rehearsal and asked me a sweet question.

"Mr. Leon, all the other kids in the show have godparents but I don't," she said. "Would you be my godfather?"

"Oh, Maria! Of course I will!"

I took it in stride, not overthinking it. But not Maria. Every now and then I'd hear from her.

"Hey, let's go see a movie! Let's go see a concert! I want to see this latest Cirque du Soleil!"

Our friendship continued like that for several years. I was a friend of the family's and her godfather. But flash ahead ten years, I'm dating her mom now.

At first, Maria was little confused.

Wait a minute! Are you still my godfather? Whoa!

She liked that we were dating but just wasn't sure what it meant.

There was a time when I didn't either.

After I got divorced from Carol, I thought about what kind of woman I wanted in my life. Should I be looking for someone to have a child with? But I had a thing for Jennifer and we'd begun seeing each other. She'd already had her family. I went with love and chose to be with someone I knew would always have my back. There was always something special about Jennifer.

Also at that time I had made a commitment not to be involved with someone in the business. I had been married to an actress. I wanted to be with someone from outside that world.

When I first met Jennifer, she ran the Virgin Islands tourist bureau, and then she was a stay-at-home mom, and then we got together. We started a foundation together and grew closer over time. Her greatest gift is her protective and maternal instinct. I loved watching how she would take care of Maria in such a loving, generous way, just like my mother and grandmother did with their children.

We started dating seriously in 2004 and got married in 2012.

All along the way, though, there was Maria and I. She would always call me when she was trying to figure out life. When she was in high school, when she was in college, when she left college and went to the London School of Economics, she would always call and we would talk through challenges she had with academics or the challenges she had in her social life and dating. We had that kind of bond. After a while, it felt like we were destined to be in the same family.

When she began to date Filip Nuytemans, my grandson Gabriel's dad, I was the first person in the family to meet Filip.

Before she introduced him to her mother and father, I met him in New York. After walking down the street for five minutes with them, I knew that they would be together.

Gabriel has two compassionate parents who really love and care for him. Filip is a general manager at Uber and they live in Amsterdam. Jennifer and I Skype with them weekly, and we travel to the Netherlands as often as we can. Being a real presence in Gabriel's life is very important to me, and I don't let the distance between us get in the way of being his grandfather.

Where Were You When the Page Was Blank?

As is clear by now, my grandmother and my mother prepared me for a life that could be whatever I wanted it to be. After I chose to pursue a life in the theater, August Wilson emerged as their professional counterpart. His work drew me to him, and working with him drew me closer not only to him, but to my grandmother and mother as well. As they had shown me so many lessons about life and living, August taught me about the creative working life. And much of what they taught me prepared me to work with August.

When I did *Joe Turner's Come and Gone* at the Alliance in September 1987, I asked August to come down during tech week and previews and give me notes. I've always been interested in knowing the playwright's intention. He was taken aback a bit.

"Oh, man. You want me to give notes? Usually directors don't ask for notes. But I'll be there."

August saw the first preview performance of *Joe Turner*. He showed up with a thick yellow legal pad, and during the show he filled that pad up.

"Damn, August!" I said. "I wanted notes but damn!"

We had a good laugh but I was really appreciative. It was beautiful to me that he took that time and he took it so seriously. That was my first glimpse of how hard August worked on his craft and how he took nothing for granted.

One of his notes from that week has remained in my directing tool kit ever since.

Joe Turner centers around a character named Herald Loomis, who had been snatched up by white people who were kidnapping and imprisoning black people. He just disappeared from his family one day. Eventually, he regains his freedom and finds his daughter. But his wife is not around. The play is essentially about Loomis trying to reunite his daughter with her mother.

Herald Loomis is a haunted, mysterious man. He's an introvert, strikes people as odd, and doesn't speak much. He's on a single-minded mission to find his wife. Throughout the play, Loomis wears a long, black coat and a hat. I was happy with how I had chosen to mount the play. In the play, Loomis, as a good Southern man with manners, is going to take off his coat and hat when he joins other people at a table to eat.

August gave me a specific note. "Don't ever have him take off that coat and hat."

I said that it just made sense for him to take them off in certain scenes.

"Don't do it," said August. "It demystifies him when you have him take off the coat and hat."

That was a beautiful note. And I made that change. August was right, and it was a strong but subtle touch. And it showed me how delicate August's work was, and I learned not to fear being courageous with the moves he put in his plays. Because leaving a black actor onstage, under hot lights, for the whole show in a big wool coat and hat is a bold move. But it worked to serve the character.

After watching the show with that change, I said to August, "I couldn't have figured that one out for myself."

August was touched that not only did I seek out his counsel, but I was not afraid to put it to work. We made that change the next day. He always liked how quickly I was willing to make changes that I found smart and creative. He liked my open, respectful, collaborative attitude.

Later on, when I did his Broadway shows, he loved the fact that, even after all those years we'd worked together, I still took his notes seriously and I always tried to get them right away.

If he said, "I'm wondering if this scene could work without his monologue..."

I'd say, "Let's try it tonight."

We would do it that night, and it would either work or not. But we'd both get to see it and make a judgment based on a real performance. I didn't go off and think about it for a few days. I was getting feedback from the author, and I valued his input immensely. This kind of collaboration with August began in 1988, but it was fully realized in 2004 when we worked on *Gem of the Ocean*.

In that play, Aunt Ester is a 285-year-old woman who is trying to heal the tortured soul of another character, Citizen Barlow. She is trying to put him at ease and she wants him to confront his past. There is a scene where she forces him to relive his "middle passage," the time in a slave's life when he or she is jammed into a crowded ship with other slaves who are traveling from Africa across the Atlantic to the West Indies.

There was also another scene with the same goal of helping Citizen deal with his past by reliving it. In this scene, August has Citizen in a pigsty eating what the hogs are eating, equating being a slave with being an animal.

One day I asked August, "What are you trying to get at with the pigpen scene?"

"I'm just trying to get at the harrowing past of this character," he said. "I think on some level we have to heal ourselves. And in order to heal ourselves, we have to accept our past and come to a beautiful understanding about where we are now."

"I'm not sure we need the scene in the pigpen."

"You think so?" he said.

"Let's try it without that scene," I said. "I think the same statement will be made by just having him relive his middle passage."

We tried it that night and August said, "You were right. Let's keep it like that."

Removing the pigpen scene also put more emphasis on the middle passage, and that scene became the anchor of the play.

To this day, I think the most sacred union is that of the writer and the director working on a new play. The process is never more beautiful and pure. When a writer works with a director, with real trust between them, they can solve any problem. Working with August on all those plays gave me the blueprint for the relationship I want to have with every writer.

With living playwrights, it's easy. But you can still do it if the playwright has passed. When I did the movie of *A Raisin in the Sun* for ABC, I took elements of Lorraine Hansberry's original screenplay that were not used in the first movie of that play. Out of respect for Lorraine, I insisted that we start our film with the Langston Hughes poem as she wanted. It helped me to understand what I always seek to understand: Why did the playwright write the play? What did she want to say?

When I worked with August, it was like trying to figure him out, get in his head, and discover why he wrote what he wrote. But he also trusted me to solve certain things. He didn't have the answers for everything and never pretended he did.

"This is what I was trying to do," he'd say. Or, "This is why I wrote that scene. This is what the scene is about." But he didn't always have every idea ready to go on how to stage the scene. And he welcomed input. And when a director is willing to work with a writer to solve things together, they will discover something that is more beautiful than just making things up that you want in the play or on the stage.

The middle passage/pigpen scenes in *Gem of the Ocean* show you how open he was. We cut a scene he had written when we *discovered together* that the one scene adequately delivered the message he was trying to deliver over two scenes.

But August wanted to hear from everybody working on a play. He wanted everybody to give as much as he gave. I use this idea to this day: if everybody pulls together and gives their all, it's the greatest form of collaboration possible.

August's point was this: I stayed up all night writing this scene.

Now I want to see the director put as much effort into the staging of the scene as I put into the writing of it. Same for the actors, set designer, lighting director, sound designer, and so on. When people did not put in the time and were not committed to the words, he'd get upset and frustrated. But I understood him so I always made sure he knew I was working as hard as he was to bring his story to life.

Whenever collaborators would complain about his work to him, August would say, "Where were you when the page was blank?"

That's another August line that I've taken to heart. I try to remember that when the writer sits down, the page is empty. And what does it take to get a life, a story, on the page? I want to spend the same kind of energy and creativity and imagination when I am trying to fill a blank stage. I feel it is my duty to match the writer's commitment.

August Wilson was the perfect example for me regarding what I wanted to be as a professional. In college, I was a political science major and a theater minor, but when theater became my work, the political side of things did not take a backseat. It was always asking me, *Why are you doing this play? Who are you trying to impact with the work?*

August came up in the revolutionary times of the 1960s and was heavily influenced by the politics of those years. He was into Amiri Baraka. We both understood the need for a play to land in a way that impacts society, but we also knew that the play can't be didactic or preachy. The work just has to breathe life into a voice that perhaps some people haven't heard. Ultimately, August wanted America to love itself, and he wanted black people to love themselves.

I've been walking proudly in August's footsteps ever since I met him. That's why I'm doing *Holler if Ya Hear Me* and not *Follies* or *Carousel*. I choose my work carefully because I think it can have an impact on our world, our young people, and our older folks.

August sacrificed a lot to write the ten plays of his *Pittsburgh Cycle*. He didn't have to do ten plays, one for each decade of the twentieth century. But once he started, he followed through. He put his blood and sweat into those plays. And it was so poetic that after he wrote that tenth play, *Radio Golf*, the spirits took him home. He was meant to do that specific work.

But he left a lot behind to help us carry on. Those ten plays mean a lot. Denzel Washington is going to produce them all for HBO. I and others will continue to direct those plays on Broadway and elsewhere. And the young kids who participate in the annual August Wilson Monologue Competition get to experience his words for themselves.

August was a complex person. I knew him for more than twenty years, but we weren't exactly buddy-buddy. Nobody really knew him completely, but he shared himself with a lot of people. He gave all of us a little piece of himself. One of the ways he'd share himself or connect with people was through storytelling.

If you saw August on the street, he'd stop you and catch up. Then he'd start telling you a story, and what you thought was going to be a five-minute encounter turned into an hour and a half. You'd start to figure out, after knowing him awhile, that he was telling you about characters or stories that he was considering for a play. He was testing out material on you. But it was always fun because he was a great, great storyteller.

One of the last few times that I spent with him, we were in the alley next to the Walter Kerr Theatre in New York. He would always go out there on the breaks to smoke. You rarely saw August without a cigarette. He's standing there, smoking away, and he says, "Hey, Kenny!" Then he launches into some of his stories.

"I'm working on this thing about a coffin builder. Check this out…"

And off he goes, and I'm just drinking it in and laughing along with him. And he spins in a little bit of world and American politics. That's who he was and that's who he inspires me to be.

August taught me about balancing commerce and art. He used to talk to me about how challenging it was to get commercial stars to do his plays. Many actors couldn't be in his plays because they always had movies and other projects lined up. He'd always say, "How many million is million enough?"

I have asked myself that question many times over. You have to have some goals and guidelines for yourself. Money can't be the only reason you take on a project. If that was the case, August would have been a millionaire ten times over.

August was always working, always thinking about people, about stories, about life. And why we do the stuff we do. That's what I mean about his sacrifice. He worked constantly to stay productive and get those ten plays done.

I know why I clicked with August, but to be honest, I don't know why he clicked with me. I think, at the beginning, my being based in Atlanta was important.

When I invited August down to visit for that first production of *Joe Turner*, he participated in one of my Lunchtime with Kenny events. I held these events in the small theater at the Alliance, which seats about 200 people. By the time word got out that the next one was with August Wilson, we had to move it to the 800-seat main theater. That day we had over 700 people bring their lunch at noon on a workday to listen to August and me talk about the upcoming production of *Joe Turner*. That was a huge moment for me and the Alliance Theatre. That's an amazing turnout for what was essentially a promotional strategy for our theater. August was blown away. He saw what we were trying to build and knew we were onto something.

Atlanta also gave August a chance to present his plays to a diverse community, which he loved. His plays usually went from Yale, where Lloyd Richards worked, to Chicago and to Los Angeles and then to Broadway. Those cities are not like Atlanta, and they are not in the South. In the back of his mind, that was important. The ten plays were about people migrating north and in that is the idea, someday for some reason, to return to the South. Watching those plays with a mixed Southern audience energized August.

The makeup of the Atlanta audience excited him in other ways, too. The lunchtime events or the shows themselves provoked a kind of laughter and engagement that those other cities did not provide. Atlanta is in the Southern Baptist Bible Belt. People talk back. They talk back a lot more than New York audiences talk back. There was a palpable sense of cultural affirmation and belonging that happened in those Atlanta shows. That was interesting to August.

Over time, I think August began to appreciate that I work fast and that I respected his notes, putting them in quickly to see what would happen. He also learned that I had utter honor and respect for the written word. I would scream at actors if they tried to paraphrase one of his lines.

Say the words as written. There is poetry in those words. If you don't want to say them as written, write your own play.

He saw that I made sure the actors worked as hard as he had.

I was also willing to experiment with him. I let him get all the ideas out of his head and onto the stage as quickly as possible. If they worked, we had solved a problem. If they didn't work, we tried something else the next day.

Gem of the Ocean was the ninth of the ten plays in August Wilson's *The Pittsburgh Cycle*. In 2004, August had called me to take over the play in Boston and deliver it to Broadway. It was only my second Broadway show, after I had done *Raisin in the Sun* earlier that same year. Just before we opened, before any reviews were in, August took me for a meal at Cafe Edison, the legendary theater district restaurant on Forty-Seventh Street in New York. He told me that the cycle was one play short of completion and he wanted me to direct that tenth play. I was a bit stunned.

Keep in mind, August was a playwright who had worked with only two other directors, Marion McClinton and Lloyd Richards. And he had won two Pulitzer Prizes along the way.

But August said he enjoyed working with me and he valued the rhythm we had established since *Joe Turner* in 1988. He wanted me for the final play in the defining series of his career.

I told him I was honored but that I had signed on to direct

Margaret Garner, an opera by Richard Danielpour with a libretto by Toni Morrison. The life of the real Margaret Garner, a runaway slave who killed her own daughter rather than let her be returned to a life of slavery, was the basis of Morrison's acclaimed novel *Beloved*. The wonderful Dr. David DiChiera, founder and artistic director of the Michigan Opera Theatre in Detroit, had asked me to direct this opera.

It was not a casual commitment.

But work on that production began at roughly the same time work would begin on August's *Radio Golf*, his monumental tenth play. I could only hope August would understand my reason for declining his offer.

August looked at me and smiled.

"A Toni Morrison opera? You gotta do that!"

Part of me couldn't believe it. August was accomplished and esteemed. His place in history had already been established. And he had a reputation for pushing for, and getting, what he wanted.

That was the first inkling I got of August's great respect for other artists. He was in full support of me working on an opera by Toni Morrison. He told me to go on and give that show my best effort. "But I may call you if I need you down the road."

August Wilson. Always generous.

One time I told August he was my hero. He exhaled some cigarette smoke and looked at me. His response reveals all you need to know about him as an artist and a man.

"Oh, man. That's a heavy burden," he said, still eyeing me. "Kenny Leon's hero? I gotta earn that."

True Colors

Back in 1991, the Alliance Theatre had received a $3 million grant from the DeWitt Wallace/Reader's Digest Foundation in recognition of our willingness to explore diversity. The head of the foundation came down to talk to the board to explain why they recognized our work so generously.

After the meeting, he mentioned he was going back to New York the next day. I said I was going there, too.

"What time does your flight leave?" I asked.

"Well, my flight leaves whenever I want it to leave."

I joined him on his plane and we started a conversation. Then he said something a bit shocking.

"Kenny, I know this is year three but what are you going to do next?"

"What do you mean?" I said. "I just got this job. I'm a black man running a major theater company in the South that is not really a black theater company. I'm diversifying it, I'm giving writers and actors jobs. I'm bringing new people into that theater."

"I disagree. I've learned in this life that every seven to ten years, you should leave a job or at least learn to make yourself over if you're going to stay in the same place. You should be thinking about that."

I thought about it and realized I'd left the Academy Theatre after about ten years. Without a plan but just because it felt right. And I got the NEA grant position, which rolled into my jobs at the Alliance. I kept his idea in the back of my mind.

In 1999 or so, coming up on my being artistic director at the Alliance for ten years, the company was looking to replace the managing director, the person with whom I would co-run the theater. I handled the creative aspect and the managing director handled the money. The closer that marriage is, the better.

The board knew that and assured me they would select someone that matched up well with me, but in the end I didn't agree with their choice, and it occurred to me that this might be a sign that it was time for me to move on.

When I took stock of my time at the Alliance, I realized that we had achieved many of our most important goals. We'd diversified the board. We'd diversified the staff, and I'd created meaningful new positions to help out, such as the community relations director, who was African American. And the work on the stage was diverse. We had developed a strong national reputation as well. I had achieved what I'd set out to do. I wasn't sure I was the one to take it further. Maybe the next artistic director needed to be a white woman or man or a Latino person to take the Alliance to the next level.

Around this time, I was on the golf course with some friends, all of whom happened to be white businessmen. I told them I was thinking about leaving my job.

"What do you mean you're leaving? You have the best job in town."

"I'm ready to move on."

"Well, give yourself a year to figure out what you are going to do next. Get that figured out and then you can leave."

The next day I went in and gave my one-year notice. It was cordial and all business. I just said it was time. And that was the truth.

It was in the paper the next day, and my golf buddies were surprised. But I told them that I didn't want to wait to set myself up and then leave. You leave when it's time as I had done at the Academy. I ended up at the Alliance for eleven years because I gave them the time to set up a national search and take care of business as they saw fit. But when I left, I did not know what was in store for me.

Not surprisingly, I began to hear from people in the theater world. I was in the running for three big jobs, including one at the Arena Stage in Washington, D.C. That didn't work out and I'm glad because I ended up with something better than I could have imagined.

Riley Temple of the Arena Stage told me I should start a national black theater company. I was hesitant because I wasn't looking to start a theater company from scratch. Then I had a great conversation with Chris Manos, an important figure in theater in Atlanta who ran Theater of the Stars and all the plays produced at the Fox Theatre.

"Kenny, we don't want you to leave Atlanta," said Chris. "You should start a company here in Atlanta that focuses on black writers and their plays."

Riley and Chris are two people I respect deeply so I listened to their advice. I still didn't want to start a theater company, but I wrote down some ideas about a theater company I'd like to run.

It would not be a black theater.

It would not be a white theater.

It would be a theater of diversity.

At the center of it, we would produce African American classics. Which is a bit of an oxymoron because if you asked what the classic African American theater works are, the only answer is *A Raisin in the Sun*. You can't name another play from the African American canon that is produced on a regular basis. And I took that as a personal challenge.

The reason was that we black artists don't revisit our work and make it fresh for a new generation. Our work has tended to be tied to whatever is happening politically and socially in the current moment. Or what is happening spiritually in the church. This condition makes theater something different in the black community than it is in the white community. Wonderful writers like James Baldwin, Zora Neale Hurston, and Leslie Lee fade in prominence because their work is not revisited and produced after they die.

The company I was contemplating would flip the model. We would produce plays by African American writers while around the edges we would diversify. We would do plays from all cultures.

But the goal would be to revive black theater by producing work by black writers so that their work could be analyzed and made relevant again by modern and updated productions.

That's how it got started, with my little manifesto. But the idea attracted serious attention. I gathered a group around me and we went to work. We would call it True Colors because it would be about truth and clarity. Later on, we decided to put my name on it because it would help us in Atlanta, where I had developed a name in the cultural community at large.

Kenny Leon's True Colors Theatre Company.

I have always been grateful to both Riley Temple and Chris Manos. They nudged me in this direction, and their faith in me is what led me to sit down that day and develop my vision for what has become True Colors.

But Chris Manos expressed his support even more forcefully. Chris truly believed in me and my idea for this company. He quietly gave me seed money to get the theater off the ground. That funding proved to be extremely important.

In the last few years, Chris has left public life. Theater of the Stars went under and he took it to heart even though the fortunes of that company were not his fault. He felt he had let the community down. He had not. What he has given to the greater Atlanta community cannot be measured. He is a wonderful and accomplished man of the arts. I learned a lot about this business from watching him. We never worked directly together, but I looked up to him from afar. I think about him every day and I miss him. When I imagine a picture of the people who helped me achieve my success in the theater, Chris Manos is prominent.

Upon giving me the money, he said, "I don't want any credit for this." I'm sorry, Chris, but this is one time I'll go against your counsel.

We started True Colors in 2001, and while the business was being put together by Jane Bishop, our cofounder, and others, I stayed busy.

I got a chance to direct *A Raisin in the Sun* and *Gem of the Ocean* on Broadway in 2004, which I could never have done if I were still running the Alliance. I did that Toni Morrison opera. Those projects started in 2003 or earlier, but I had freed myself to accept opportunities like them.

The first production of Kenny Leon's True Colors Theatre Company was in October 2003.

Fences by August Wilson.

I asked August to come to Atlanta to help us give birth to this theater based on ideas and convictions I'd learned from him.

August came down to celebrate with us. His voice was a little hoarse. All those cigarettes. But he walked onto the stage and toasted our company into existence.

He blew life into Kenny Leon's True Colors Theatre Company in 2003 just as he and his work had invigorated my life and work in 1987. And the True Colors Theatre Company would be the home of my effort to keep August's work and spirit alive in our country and culture.

I Don't See What They Is to Enjoy

When I did *T Bone N Weasel* at the Alliance in 1988, Grandma Mamie came to see the show.

The play is a comedy about a black guy and a white guy who break out of jail. I was nervous because it was rare for someone on an NEA fellowship to get a chance to direct. We were in the small 300-seat theater, and I'd say the audience was about 99 percent white. During the first act, you could clearly hear someone talking.

"Uh-huh, baby. No, don't do that. Uh-huh, baby."

It's my grandmother.

She's reacting and speaking out loud because of the traditions of the Southern Baptist Church. She has never been to the theater but it's a similar setting, an audience and a stage. She figures, "I'll just act the way I do in church." It's a beautiful thing.

At intermission, several board members and people in the audience came to me and said, "Who is that woman talking?"

"That's my grandma Mamie," I said. "Don't mess with her."

For the second act, everybody was back in their seats and the lights went up. Once the play started up again, you could hear a chorus of voices.

"Oh no, baby. Don't do that! Uh-huh!"

Instead of just my grandmother, you had 300 people responding like that to the play. It was even more beautiful than when she did it alone. It was a great example of the power of integration. This is what happens when black sits next to white. Or when nonreligious sits next to religious. We rub off on each other. And our worlds get bigger.

When I talk about diversity and inclusion, I always remember that performance and my grandmother's natural, honest response. She took herself wherever she went.

If something is good, she lets you know. If something is bad, she lets you know.

That audience loved that show and having Grandma in the audience with them. By the time it was over, they'd had a brand-new theater experience. They hadn't ever felt free to let their voices ring out to the actors. There was clapping in unusual places, too. They had been liberated by her example and they loved it.

I have the same reaction when I go to the symphony. I want to clap and shout at the end of a movement but that doesn't fit the culture of classical music. At the symphony, I know how my grandmother felt at that play. She brought herself to that play and gave everyone present a night to remember fondly.

The second play she saw was *Fences*. The show was on the main stage at the Alliance, with about 800 people in the audience. At intermission, I went to her seat to see how she was doing. It's important to remember just how much she meant to me. I was so proud of her, so grateful for all she had done for me. Here she was, in this world she knew I would find without knowing about it herself. Her prayer for me. I wanted to find out how it was all coming across to her.

"Grandma Mamie, are you enjoying the show?"

"Well, I don't see what they is to enjoy."

In retrospect, I see that *Fences* was too much a mirror of her own life. Everything that I *recognized* in the play, she *felt*. I was mesmerized and inspired by the language and the portrayal of life as I really knew it. I didn't connect as strongly to the plot and the characters' decisions because I never forgot it was a play, a fiction. But Mamie didn't actually separate real life from the play, and the story disturbed her.

This is horrible. He's not treating his son right and he's down the street with this other woman and got her pregnant. I don't see what they is to enjoy.

Grandma Mamie was glad to see my work. But the sharply drawn world that August created was too close to home. She couldn't separate the pain onstage from pain she herself had known, from heartache, racism, and the harshness of her times.

I have never forgotten that conversation with Grandma Mamie. From that night on, I have tried to keep a very thin line between what is onstage and what feels raw and honest. Once we set the tone, it has to be real the rest of the way. I don't want to see a lot of performing. I don't want to see any acting. I want to see people disappear into that world.

If the audience sees the play as real, what they see onstage can reach a deeper level of honesty. You can't fake your way through that. You can truly touch people if you create a world they believe in.

If you look at all of my work, you'll see that quality consistently. My shows are a search for truth presented onstage in a way that people perceive as truthful. The style or genre varies. But whether it's a romantic comedy or a drama, we are going for truth and we're going for everybody being in the same story. If everybody onstage is in the same story, the audience joins them. And then you can create the idea in the theater that "This is real. This is honest."

Grandma Mamie was telling me that the show was working as I'd intended. Her feedback is what all great work can generate and I'm referring to August. The specificity of his writing creates a universal bond and leads to understanding and feeling. In many ways, August is like Shakespeare. If someone does Shakespeare really well, then everyone can receive it. The same is true of August's work.

August took a specific African American story, that of Southerners going north, that journey about being present and accounted for in this country, and wrote about it in a way no one else ever has. For the first time, we heard our ancestors and saw our connections to our whole community and its history.

And those ten plays are very American plays. As such, they allow my grandmother to find herself in August's America and, by extension, allow me to find myself in America, too. We are not on the outside looking in. His plays are not from the white master's point of view but from a voice that says, "This is our story, our history, our inner life and spirit as we have grown and evolved in America. This is what it was like."

So Grandma Mamie found herself there. She did love the musicality of the language and the overall portrayal of the characters even though it was African Americans in Pittsburgh. August's artistry allowed her to find her true Southern, Florida self in the play. Grandma Mamie would have found herself in *The Piano Lesson*, too, especially in Boy Willie's speech about wanting to sell the piano to buy some farmland. There are a lot of similarities between that speech, that play, and how my grandmother grew up.

Just as August Wilson's plays reminded me of my grandmother and her world before I was born, August Wilson himself reminded me of my grandma Mamie. You'd sit down with either one of them and start to talk, and the next thing you know, it's an hour later. August would be testing out his ideas, seeing how you react to the stories from the play he's working on. My grandma would tell you stories about her life in everyday conversation. You'd think it's just another one of Grandma's stories. But no, it would be about us, and her, and her younger self and her cousins.

Her reasons would not be as obvious as August's, but she had them. She spun her stories so that we would know our past and so that we might learn from it. She wanted us to know that we weren't that far removed from hard times. She took the responsibility to impart values to us in her stories. She also wanted us to appreciate stories and storytelling. I know that listening to her prepared me for my work in the theater.

Stories are everywhere.

The Ground on Which He Stood

In April 2005, I was running the True Colors Theatre Company and taking advantage of opportunities to develop my craft and spread the word about our theater, much as I had when I was at the Alliance.

As I had told August Wilson I would, I went to Detroit and worked on *Margaret Garner* while his *Radio Golf* went into production. The play opened at the Yale Repertory Theatre in New Haven, Connecticut, in April 2005. August called me after opening night and said, "Well, that didn't go as I wanted it to. Can you come and take over now?" I had another month of work to go before the premiere of *Margaret Garner*, but how could I say no to such a flattering offer from the most important professional influence in my life? I said yes and we worked something out.

I went to New Haven and took the play over. The plan was to go to Los Angeles for a run at the Mark Taper Forum. Which we did. But in June 2005, August was diagnosed with inoperable liver cancer and given five months to live, and that's how long he lasted.

In that summer of 2005, I worked on *Radio Golf* in Los

Angeles. On Mondays, I'd fly up to Seattle to be with August. I'd sit on the porch and talk to him and Todd Kreidler, August's dramaturge and closest friend in the world.

One afternoon, after spending the previous day and that morning with August, Todd and I went out to a bar around three o'clock. We both knew it was serious with August and that we'd likely lose him very soon. We were both upset and didn't want to be alone. We were in no mood to sleep either, and I think we went home at three or four the next morning. We sat there, in this brown room, and watched it go from being a bar to a restaurant to a pickup club to a dance club. We finally stumbled out of there and ate early-morning hot dogs on the street before parting.

Over those long hours in that bar, Todd and I confronted our impending loss. We wanted to think of a way to keep August alive. The best way was to keep his work alive. As theater people, we both knew that Shakespeare monologue competitions were popular events. We felt August was our Shakespeare. The National August Wilson Monologue Competition was born that night.

My friendship with Todd Kreidler goes back to the development and production of August's ninth play, *Gem of the Ocean*. It was early in 2003, and August had just started working on the show. I got a call from Marion McClinton, who had replaced the retired Lloyd Richards as August's main director. They were casting it out of New York.

At that point, I was a known actor but I had been shifting my focus to directing. I had directed almost all of August's plays somewhere in the country, but I'd never worked as an actor with

August. And I'd never done commercial theater with his work, only regional.

Marion's idea was to cast me as Citizen Barlow, one of the main characters in the play. Marion said he'd run it by August but to plan to come to Chicago for an initial run at the Goodman Theatre. I felt blessed to be able to work with August in this way, to be part of his process of writing, rewriting, arranging, and rearranging a play. I'd only worked with him as a director on plays he had finished. But *Gem of the Ocean* was still taking shape. While working on that show, I met Todd. I saw firsthand how close he was to August and how involved he was in his writing.

I left the show and went back to my work in Atlanta, but I was grateful to Marion and August for the experience. In 2004, August called me to work on *Gem* again, and I thought he was asking me to return as an actor, but by then I really considered myself a full-time director.

They were still working on the play and were up in Boston.

"We need you," he said. "Marion is ill and we need a director. But things are crazy. It's not smooth sailing. We need you to come in and get this ship pointed in the right direction." By which he meant "get us to Broadway."

After all he'd done for me, refusing August was not an option. But I was also pretty busy. I had directed *Raisin in the Sun* on Broadway earlier in 2004 so this would be my second Broadway show and second one that year. And I was doing a True Colors show in Washington, D.C., that was in a bit of turmoil. I explained it all to August and he said he could work around whatever schedule worked best for me. For two weeks, I directed two plays every day. Rehearse all day in Boston. Fly to D.C. and rehearse that show. Sleep. Rehearse again in D.C. Fly to Boston. Rehearse. But it all worked out because soon August said, "We're ready. Let's go to Broadway!"

After that stretch, I learned from August that I could push myself through any professional challenges. If I think the show is worth it, I can dig deep and find what I need.

During these couple of years, I worked very closely with August and Todd together. As I've said, August was demanding and Todd was not spared. While he did get the coffee and cigarettes when asked, he wasn't really that kind of an assistant. He assisted August in every respect. Whatever August needed in a writing partner, researcher, or friend, Todd delivered. August respected Todd and loved teaching him about writing. The only thing August wanted for Todd was for him to take all he'd learned and go out and make it on his own as a writer, which he has, with a thriving career writing for the stage, movies, and television.

When August passed away, there was a void for both of us. Todd had lost his best friend and mentor. And I had lost the most important professional influence of my career, just after taking that relationship to new levels by acting for him and directing one of his shows on Broadway. August's funeral completed my bond with my brother Todd.

Todd was in charge of executing August's meticulous plans for his funeral, the final act of devotion between them. The service took place, of course, in Pittsburgh. The site was the Soldiers & Sailors Memorial Hall & Museum.

August chose his pallbearers, who included Todd and me.

There were to be three speakers at the funeral—Marion McClinton, Todd, and me. August wanted the funeral procession to travel through the Pittsburgh he'd immortalized in his writing, and we made our way through the Hill District, where all of August's plays except *Ma Rainey's Black Bottom* take place. Phylicia Rashad performed a piece from *Gem of the Ocean*. Wynton Marsalis played "Danny Boy."

August wanted us all to eat corn bread and drink whiskey as he had done so many times in the Hill District. They buried August right next to his mother. It was a sad, rainy day in Pittsburgh. I can still hear the mud as it slipped and dropped with a thud onto the casket after we lowered him into the ground.

"You will not be a footnote in American history," I said in my eulogy. "We guarantee the young kids will know who August Wilson is."

In addition to his plays, August wrote a tour de force essay in which he stated his artistic purpose. Delivered as the keynote speech at the Theatre Communications Group's eleventh biennial conference, *The Ground on Which I Stand* is required reading for all Americans who care about cultural diversity and why it matters.

> So much of what makes this country rich in art and all manners of spiritual life is the contributions that we as African Americans have made. We cannot allow others to have authority over our cultural and spiritual products. We reject, without reservation, any attempt by anyone to rewrite our history so as to deny us the

rewards of our spiritual labors, and to become the cultural custodians of our art, our literature and our lives. To give expression to the spirit that has been shaped and fashioned by our history is of necessity to give voice and vent to the history itself.

—August Wilson

V.

Wilsonian Soldiers

A short time after August died, I was looking for an associate artistic director at True Colors. My dear friend Narda Alcorn was August's stage manager for many years and knew I had this opening.

"Does your associate have to be an African American?" she asked. True Colors was technically a company devoted to the preservation of African American classics so her question was fair.

"No. It just has to be a person who understands the importance of African American literature and how relevant and meaningful it is to the whole of America."

"Well, you and Todd are such great friends," she said. "You both are missing August terribly. What about him for the job?"

I knew instantly that she was right and named Todd our associate artistic director. He stayed for five years, and we did wonderful things together. And on a personal level, we helped each other grieve. And we helped each other fulfill the promise we had made to each other, and to August, in that brown room in Seattle just before August died.

We started the National August Wilson Monologue Competition in 2007 at Tri-Cities High School in Atlanta. Today, the competition is truly national as we have regional competitions in twelve cities from Boston to Seattle, and we have the finals in New York at the August Wilson Theatre.

The first year, we went into that high school and explored the plays with the kids and asked them to compete using any monologue they wanted. Every year, we added another school from the Atlanta area.

Early on, True Colors and I would raise about $200,000 for all the kids to be together one weekend in Atlanta. I would do an hour workshop with them about career building. I'd try to get a celebrity in every year to talk to the kids and or be a judge. I'd recruit actors, producers, directors, and designers who'd worked on August's plays.

As we head into our second decade with the competition, I take the stage at the August Wilson Theatre hosting the national finals and teaching as well. It's like a master class except 500 or 600 hundred people are watching.

My main message is for the kids to embrace the values that August discussed in his plays: pride in citizenship, pride in country, pride in your culture. Claiming your place as an American citizen. We started it all in that one school, and we have spread it across the country based on personal connections and friendships with theater professionals who believe in August's work as deeply as we do.

During the finals weekend, I want the kids to put a face on dreams. Put a face on success. Put a face on what's possible. Over the course of the weekend, whether they got a chance to touch the hand of Denzel Washington or to talk to his wife, Pauletta, or to spend time with Ruben Santiago-Hudson, who has a TV show that they watch every week on BET, *The Quad*, I want them to be close to success and successful people.

They know my story because I tell them.

"Kenny Leon grew up with his stepfather and mother in a household making about ten thousand dollars a year. But now he's doing Broadway shows and he's doing live television specials for NBC. He's doing everything I want to do."

I want them to know that story so they'll know success comes from within. I went from Miccosukee Road to Broadway. I'm not a special Negro. I'm not a magic Negro. That journey is possible for each and every one of them, too.

I want them to know that it takes a lot of hard work but it's worth it.

I want them to know that life is not fair. There is racism. August Wilson left school because a teacher didn't believe that he, as a black student, had done his homework. I win a Tony Award, but do I get the same opportunities after that as white directors who win a Tony? No. Absolutely not. It might not be direct racism, but it's racism just the same. Still, I tell them, don't go through life complaining that there is racism. Do something about it. Take responsibility for your life. Do something about all the roadblocks out there. It can be done. Live life on your terms. And yes, take you wherever you go.

Some of them are stuck in their communities and are a bit timid about what lies ahead. But when they leave that weekend, I want them to go home and dream fully. To say, "You know what? Any damn thing is possible."

Each year I ask the kids to be Wilsonian soldiers, to take on August's ideas and keep them alive by performing his work and helping us keep him alive. I give them permission every year to call me Uncle.

"For the rest of your life, I'm your Uncle Kenny. That means I may sneak up behind you when you're in college in Detroit, Michigan, or San Francisco, California. I'll say, 'What are you doing? What are you doing out after twelve? Nothing good happens after twelve. How is your education coming? How are your dreams coming? What are you doing to be the best person you can be?' I'll be that person, along with these other Wilsonian soldiers. We're going to haunt you the rest of your life to make sure you're turning out to be great citizens.

"If you embrace this and become true Wilsonian soldiers, you'll go to your colleges and demand that August Wilson's ten plays be taught in the curriculum. If you pursue acting in school, you'll demand that your teachers present his plays. You'll be passing on this great writer and encouraging the next generation to embrace him."

At the end of the night, we give them the boxed set of all ten plays and the top three winners get scholarship money. All the competitors, around twenty kids give or take, have had a trip to New York, seen a Broadway show with me, stood on a Broadway stage, mingled with successful theater people, and taken a master class in acting and life lessons. But every year I'm the one who gets the most out of the competition.

Each year I am reminded anew of August's achievement. These young students never fail to show me another layer of his depth and humanity and his all-important universality.

One year a young white lesbian performed a monologue by Bynum Walker from *Joe Turner's Come and Gone*. She told me that she identified with Bynum because Bynum is an odd character and people looked at him differently because he was into conjuring and putting spells on people. She felt that people looked at her that way, too. She connected with this character strongly despite how little they seemed to have in common.

She's white, he's black.

She's young, he's old.

She's gay, he's straight.

Yet forty years ago, August put pen to paper in such a way that here in the next century a young woman is finding herself in that play. Bynum represented the universal truth of the outsider, and this young woman was drawn to him because she sensed that she was an outsider, too. Her performance of the monologue was beautiful, and she imbued it with her own meaning while keeping Bynum present, too.

That woman's performance is why I keep doing this work. To see this great artist's work come alive in the minds of all these young kids. It demonstrates clearly that we are all simply part of a process of living and of giving. August's plays continue to give. I see that every year.

The monologue performances of these young people, mostly untrained or inexperienced actors, allow me as a professional director to sit back and listen to the pure poetry of the text. Any kind of performance idea disappears and what's left are just the words and August's intention when he wrote them.

For those two hours onstage with these amazing kids, I get a chance to reflect as an artist and to understand at a greater, deeper level why I do what I do. I hear these very familiar lines and passages as though for the first time. It rejuvenates me. In a surprising yet very real way, this competition helps me become a better director.

By giving, I receive.

Prayers Are an Exchange between Generations

As I've said, the thoughts, prayers, and actions of my family elders, especially my grandmother and mother, made my life possible. Their focus on a better life for me and my siblings was the driving force in my life until I was able to take control and make my own choices, guided by them, of course.

They drilled it into me.

You can do what you want. And the best way to get what you want, and to be happy having it, is to be yourself. You have what you need within you. It's always been there.

As I've grown, however, I have seen that prayers go both ways. I have seen my generation wish for better things for our parents once we became capable of helping them. My grandmother lived to be eighty-seven, and I certainly prayed for her peace, health, and happiness along the way. I also gave prayers of thanks that my grandmother's life, after she turned forty, got quite a bit easier. She didn't live a life of luxury nor did she seek one. But her life, after the farm, was a bit lighter and reflected more of what she wanted rather than what she *had* to do.

KENNY LEON

I've seen the power of prayer and I believe in it. I also believe that I have to carry on in my grandmother's and mother's way of helping the next generation to better themselves as they grow. I know how much the messages and prayers aimed at me were worth. I've made a point of passing them on, in my life and in my work.

I worked with Ariana Grande in 2016 on *Hairspray Live!* for NBC. In our culture, celebrity delivers advance information. So I knew about Ariana but I didn't know Ariana. At the time, she was the hottest twenty-three-year-old the country had seen in a long time. I'd seen her on TV and in advertising, read mentions in the press. Would she be a diva? Would she have a posse? Would this all work out? I didn't know what to expect. The negotiations with Ariana had the usual ups and downs but eventually she signed on. We never really thought about anyone else.

I met Ariana the first time at the table read at the beginning of rehearsal and then everyone went away for a while. It was only one day but I had a good feeling. The cast got to meet one another as we read the script and sang the songs. Ariana seemed to fit in and was excited to be involved. We'd have a solid two months of rehearsal leading to the live broadcast on NBC on December 7, 2016.

On the first day of our actually working together, in early October, on the back lot at Universal Studios, I said to her, "I don't know what your expectations are for this, but I have no agenda other than having this be a memorable time for you. I have something I want you to think about. When a successful person takes a professional risk, it draws attention.

"What do you wanna do?"

She said, "I want to take acting seriously. I think that I'm a full artist."

I said, "OK. You wanna do this seriously. When you step out of your lane, that's when you have to set an example. That's when you have to be a leader. Be there on time. Work really hard and I will work with you to help you reach your goals."

I think she appreciated that, and from that day on, there was never anything star-ish about Ariana. She was on time for the whole run. She worked hard in rehearsal and was open to direction. And because there were a lot of other people in the show who were her age but who weren't major, major stars, she had to be a model for the ensemble when it came to doing the work. And she took that very seriously. I watched her set the right example every day, spending time with people she didn't know, being approachable, being a professional and a good colleague.

Ariana knew her lines and did beautiful work. And I did my part, working with her and helping her as an actor. We became friendly over time and kept chattin' it up.

"Ariana, you should do Broadway someday."

"Oh, I want to, I want to!"

As we got to know each other, I start seeing that she had much more to offer the world than she'd shown. I became a fan of hers. It was like that with the whole cast. We all bonded. Kristin Chenoweth, Jennifer Hudson, Ariana, Dove Cameron, Harvey Fierstein, Martin Short, they all got really close to one another. Ariana accepted the challenge of taking it seriously and understanding that she had to learn to do something that she usually doesn't spend her time on. I appreciated her attitude and effort. It would have made my job pretty hard, with all these seasoned actors, if Ariana had mailed it in or tried to sneak by on her voice and her fame.

Another thing we learned working on *Hairspray* was how we can help one another generationally. With the right mind-set, learning is possible no matter who's the teacher and who's the student.

For instance, Ariana and the younger cast members were hippin' me up about Instagram, Twitter, and social media in general. During breaks, they would share stuff with me and volunteer their take on it all. They said, "Twitter is like a business tool but Instagram is a more personal way to connect."

I was already on Twitter so I understood what they meant. People who know you for theater may not know you in the pop world. But then they see you're connected to Sam Jackson or Academy Awards show producers Craig Zadan and Neil Meron (also producers of *Hairspray Live!*). They see the connections and figure, *Maybe the theater might not be as boring and stuffy as I thought*. It helps people see your career and professional world in a new way.

Still, I couldn't understand Instagram.

"But, Ariana, Instagram is just taking pictures of where you are."

She said, "Yes, but it allows people to sort of hang out with you. They can't travel to where you are but they can experience it through you. You may be in Missouri on a river and we can see.

"Oh, look, Kenny is in Missouri on a river!

"We not only get to know what you're doing but we can see what you're about and what kind of things you do and places you visit. We see what you like and what matters to you. And we actually get to *see* it. Images, photos, and video sort of work better for our generation than written pieces or descriptions. Social media is about seeing things, not necessarily reading things.

"Kenny Leon, we have to get you on Instagram!"

I agreed and they helped me set up my account. Once I got on Instagram, Ariana told me, "I like the way you take your selfies. Your picture is always down at the lower end of the screen. That's really hip. That's unique. You should kinda, sorta always do that so people get to know: that's Kenny."

So, while working on *Hairspray*, generations were going back and forth, helping each other. That's a goal of any production I work on. I certainly have a better understanding of the nuances of social media and how I can use them. And I got some fresh ideas on how to reach a younger audience.

During our rehearsals for *Hairspray Live!*, Donald Trump won the election for president of the United States. During that last month before the election, some people involved with *Hairspray Live!* were concerned about where the country was going and how the climate in the country seemed to be getting a bit hostile to minorities of all kinds. Ariana and some of the other younger folks were looking to me for some guidance. And the day after Trump won, Ariana said to me, "Kenny, you got to talk to us! We need a pep talk!"

At rehearsal that morning, I looked at everyone in the cast, especially the younger ones. As we gathered, I thought, *What do I say?* I'm sure I had a poem that I had already planned to share, but the moment called for more.

"Our country is stronger than one person," I said. "We have a nation of checks and balances. And the people that are gonna make the difference are you guys! The young folks will. Any kind of progress that has happened in this country is because of the youth. Your conviction and leadership matter a great deal.

"We're doing this play on live television *about integration and inclusion.* We have an opportunity to really affect the world, too. We'll be sharing that story and showing them, reminding them, why we chose *Hairspray* in the first place. The forces that led to this election result are why we're doing *Hairspray.*"

It's disguised as this fun, humorous musical, but the show really is about that scene when Ariana's character, Penny, has found the love of her life in Seaweed but he's from another race. She's white and he's black. They go to Motormouth's place and she reminds them that they are part of an ongoing, real struggle in our society.

When Jennifer Hudson, as Motormouth, sings, "I Know Where I've Been," she is reminding them of exactly what I reminded the cast of that morning before rehearsal.

There's a light in the darkness
Though the night is black as my skin
There's a light burning bright
Showing me the way
But I know where I've been

You've got to know your past. You've got to understand the power that you have and what you must do in fragile times. The culmination of the show and its message is that song. We used the show itself to help us. We used all of that feeling and emotion to help ourselves get past the election result and what it might signify.

My message was we need to perform *Hairspray Live!* to the best of our abilities. Now more than ever.

Knowing you have that power in you makes the obstacles and hurdles in life easier to handle. Everything we did in *Hairspray Live!*, all the work we put in, was for that scene.

In December and January, after *Hairspray Live!*, as happens on most shows, people from the show and I stayed in touch. It's an odd feeling, to be apart after being together all those days and doing tremendous things together. You're still in contact but not going in to work anymore. For a while, you don't know what to do. It's part of the business and something you have to work through.

For the next several months, Ariana and I kept in decent contact. Texting, Instagram. Checking in kind of stuff. She had started her Dangerous Woman tour and would be coming to Atlanta on April 12.

We spoke and she asked me to come to the show even though she claimed my presence would make her nervous. I didn't believe her. And of course I'd be at the show.

I took a friend and his daughter to the show and we had a blast. We visited Ariana backstage and had a really nice visit.

As we got up to leave, I told Ariana, "Thanks for such a great night! I really love you."

"I really love you, too, Kenny," said Ariana as we embraced. "And I'm off to Europe in two weeks!"

"All right," I said. "Go ahead now. Do your thing."

About five weeks after that amazing night in Atlanta, I was home relaxing. My phone rang, and it was the friend who had gone to the show with me. He said, "Did you check in on Ariana?"

"What do you mean?" I said.

"The details are scarce right now but there was a bombing at the end of her concert tonight in England. You need to see how she's doing."

I texted her something casual. What's up? I just wanted to let her know I was available.

Ariana texted back pretty quickly. I'm terrified. What's wrong with the world? I'm just sobbing and I'm scared! This is such an evil thing. I don't know what to do.

I didn't really know the specifics of what had happened. There wasn't a lot out there yet. I did my best to calm her. I told her that, yes, it was a terrible thing that had happened but that she was part of the solution. Don't retreat. Reach out to others and go toward love.

"Don't let hate win. Somehow, you have to find your voice. Your voice has to add to the love. Love always wins."

As everyone knows now, Ariana was giving a concert in Manchester, England, on May 22, 2017. A terrorist set off a suicide bomb as the concert was ending, killing twenty-two people and injuring sixty or more.

Ariana is my friend, but my role is to be a paternal figure, to look out for her and offer advice and help. This moment was more serious than anything I ever thought I would talk to her about, but that's life. She needed me, and others, right now. My instinct was to support and help her. Others were in touch with Ariana that night, but I was glad to be able to do my part and send her the love and encouragement she needed.

Ariana was undoubtedly shaken in the moment and for several days afterward. Scared and upset. Anyone would be. But I know that she came back to herself and gathered her strength pretty quickly. An important part of it all was the hundreds of people she must have heard from in those early days. People reaching out to her to give her the strength to reach out to others. Funny how that works.

In the days after the attack, I would wake up and think of her. I would text her messages of support. You are one of the most powerful artists in the world and I believe in you.

Or I'd just say, Thinking of you.

Or I'd say other things that I knew she would respond to. Your work, your artistry is your tool. That's your power. They can't take that away from you. People need you. We need you in the world now more than anything.

While working on *Hairspray Live!*, Ariana and I had often talked about the responsibility of the artist to promote love and understanding and to see and accept that artists can impact the world. She was being called on to be do just that, and I was glad that we had the foundation to be able to talk about those kinds of things. I only had to reinforce what she already knew.

Ariana and her team decided that the best response was to go back to Manchester and put on the *One Love Manchester* benefit concert. I was very proud of how she handled it all. She went right back to the scene of the horror, but she did it as she moved toward love, taking many people with her and helping them heal. Love won again.

I watched that June 5 concert live on television. I texted her, That's what you do and that's how you do it. So proud of you. The next day she was visiting people in the hospital. Ariana was out there among people who were hurting and showing them she cared. Her response was perfect.

I have never been so proud of another human being in my life. Her response to that tragedy was an example of my grandmother's advice that is the title of this book. *Take You Wherever You Go.* After someone tried to use her fame and success to make their own negative and destructive point, Ariana would not allow it to be the last word. She went back, in her full power, and showed the world that violence is not an answer. She took herself back to Manchester, and she showed that she was not cowed or defeated, and in doing so, she began the physical and spiritual recovery from the tragedy. She went back to where she had been before the explosion and finished what she had started. She prevailed. And in doing so, showed others that they can, too.

Ariana Grande never met my grandma Mamie. But I think they would have gotten along.

Am I Getting Better?

In theater, television, and movies, one of the biggest motivations is *the next project*. In my particular area of show business, you get a job and that's great. You work very hard for months on a play for Broadway. But once it opens, the director's job is over. You need to plan and pursue your next job, and you start that before the current job ends. It's very cyclical. And you need to know yourself and what you like to do. You can't just take anything. You need goals and targets. Over time, I've developed a way to filter out distractions and focus on what I want to accomplish with a show. Or with an actor.

When I was casting *Hairspray Live!*, pretty early on I knew I wanted Jennifer Hudson for the role of Motormouth Maybelle. At the time, in 2016, Jennifer was performing as Shug Avery in *The Color Purple* on Broadway. I asked my friends and frequent producers of my work, including *Hairspray Live!*, Craig Zadan and Neil Meron, to see if they could set up a meeting for me with Jennifer. They did. Craig and Neil wanted Jennifer, too, so if the conversation went well, she was in.

After we chatted awhile, I got down to my main point.

"Jennifer, I've seen everything you have done." I said. "I'm a huge fan of yours. But I happen to think that you are just scratching the surface of what you can give to the world as an artist. I see directors have used you in a particular way. *Jennifer has this God-given voice and talent for singing. Let's just hear her sing.* And I understand that. But I also see that you have more to offer.

"*Hairspray* is all about Motormouth's son. The racism he encounters and the resistance to his dating a white girl. The emotional center of the show is Motormouth's song to her son. You and I would be the highest-ranking black people in this production. What we have in common is that we know and understand the history of our people in this country. We've both had loss in our lives. I miss my grandmother every day, and so much of what I do is in tribute to all she went through and what she gave me.

"Just remember why we are doing *Hairspray*. It's a gift to your son.

"If you join the show, remember that when you sing 'I Know Where I've Been,' you're singing it with the help of the two hundred million other folks that have died, white and black, for the struggle. And you're singing it for Dr. King and Rosa Parks and Joseph Lowery and Malcolm X. For your family and my grandma Mamie. We're all singing it for them. All of it is part of a process from the time we set foot in this country through slavery, through civil rights, and up to now. The challenges continue as we both know.

"No one on the show may understand it on the level that we do. But I promise that if you work with me, I will work with you to make sure your character is rock solid. Your performance will lead into that song, and it will be so transformative that both of us will never forget it.

"I also want you to know that I don't want you to really even go there until the night of the live performance. I don't have to see you try to repeat it in rehearsals. But on *that* night, know that you're singing this with all the ancestors helping you."

Very quickly in that conversation, Jennifer and I found a commonality. We talked about family, church, spirituality. I told her about Grandma Mamie and she told me about her family. We talked about how we feel that there are no accidents in life. We talked about what we want to achieve in our work. And for each of those subjects, we discovered that we agreed, that we saw so many things the same way. She was in.

The night of the live telecast, I whispered in her ear, "Hey, this is the night. Do it for us. Do it for all of us."

Jennifer was as good as Motormouth Maybelle as I could have hoped. Leading up to the live broadcast, she had done incredible work, and Craig and Neil said to me more than once, "Oh, she's killin' it."

But I knew in my heart she had another level to go.

And on that night, if you look at the tape, you can see she delivered a performance that surprised people she had been working with on the song for the previous two months. There's a moment when she slips out of frame, not desirable in a live television performance, because the cameraman was startled or reeling from what he saw and heard. He lost her for a second. That's not a criticism either. He was in the moment and was caught up. There were many moments in the song when Jennifer hit a deep place in her soul as she connected to the words and their meaning to her. Her artistry and humanity took that song to a place it had never been before, with all due respect to previous singers of it. Like a superior athlete, she reached down at the right moment for just a little more and produced something beautiful and stunning, which was just a bit deeper and more powerful than she had done with the song before.

Look at Ariana Grande or Dove Cameron in that scene. You can see all the young people look at her in a bit of awe.

"Oh my God! She has gone somewhere we haven't seen her go! And we thought we knew where she was going!"

That was such a special moment for the young performers to witness. How to give your all when you rehearse. And then find a little bit more in that final, live performance.

That show, and that electric performance, will always hold a special place in my heart. To this day, I feel very close to her even after just one experience. I think it meant a lot to Jennifer, too. And the song has become part of her repertoire. We are trying to find a way to work together again because of the *Hairspray* experience. It was perfect bonding of director, actor, and trust.

I believe that our conversation in her *Color Purple* dressing room was on target. The depth of her acting was greater than I'd seen before. She brought a three-dimensional quality to Motormouth. The connection between the spoken words and the song was clear. They were one. She also tapped into her sexuality and charisma. This woman she was playing was very sensual and had great presence. She was full of confidence. And she was a maternal figure but not a traditional mother. She had a boldness that Jennifer captured and delivered.

That performance unleashed a great artist. Jennifer was a force to be reckoned with just as Motormouth is. She drew on her life and applied it to the character and created something that was separate from herself. It was something created out of the universe combined with pinches of little things from her life experiences.

At this point in my career, I feel I can spot in other artists what I saw in Jennifer that had not yet been tapped. I saw an exciting part of her talent, and heart, that the world hadn't seen yet. I sensed she had somewhere else to go.

All the great ones do.

They want to go where they haven't gone before. They want to get better.

Great actors don't tell you they want to get better. They show you in their actions and their work ethic.

When I work with Phylicia Rashad, inevitably she will ask me, "What time do we get out of rehearsal because I have a voice lesson right after?"

Denzel Washington is not afraid to say, "Can we rehearse that scene again? Can we keep working on this?"

And Sam Jackson has no trouble saying, "What are you talking about, motherfucker? Make yourself clear."

Sam's question is a demand for the director to know what he's talking about and to be able to articulate precisely where he wants the actor to go.

Actors often deal with directors who can't do that. They encourage the actors to do what they've done before, to use what they bring to the part, not to find something new.

But the best performances are a partnership between the actor and the director, and the great actors want and understand that. They want to understand what you think they are capable of doing, and they want you to know where they think they are capable of going.

Phylicia might want to take her character to a higher level and figure out a way to tie her spirituality into her creation of a character.

Denzel may want you to help him investigate a backstory of Troy Maxson in *Fences* that's different from a conversation he would have with any other director.

The great ones want to explore every part of their being so they know the character as well as they know themselves. They want to know the director is paying attention to that process.

As a director, you let actors know you are paying attention to their work and their process by the questions you ask and the environment you create. You must have a place where they are not afraid to be shitty. Even the most accomplished veteran actors can stumble on their way to finding a role. They have to be comfortable in their search and willing to try new things until they find what works. They have to know they have your support and trust.

Working with Kristin Chenoweth on *Hairspray* was a great experience for me as a director. I want to work with her again. That woman has something to offer that we have not seen, a quality that always draws me to an actor.

I'm sure Helen Mirren, with whom I'm dying to work, is the

same way. Morgan Freeman. Ian McKellen. All the great ones think like that. They want to be tested, stretched. They want to show you they can do something you haven't seen them do before. That's where their greatness lives.

The same impulse drives me.

Not long ago, I woke up, got out of bed, and told my wife, "I'm not joking here. But my greatest work has yet to happen."

I was watching *The Godfather* recently. That movie is ageless and so beautifully made. It is filled with iconic shots and dialogue. We've all seen the part where Sonny Corleone is shot to death at the toll booth. But each time I see it, I am drawn in. They stay on that bullet-ridden car, with Sonny draped on it, for a long time. And you can't look away, no matter how many times you have seen it.

The director, Francis Ford Coppola, also made powerful use of ritual, a wedding or a birth. We all relate to it instantly. The story of *The Godfather* is about all the values we hold dear as American families. The film is not about the Mafia. The world of the Mafia is the setting for Coppola to tell a lasting, human, and American story. His artistry allowed him to make a film of enduring quality that has withstood the test of time.

I would like to do work that has that kind of long-lasting impact. With live theater, the work lives on in the memories of the audience. I did a production of *Our Town* a few years ago, and people still come up to me today and say, "I loved what you did with *Our Town*. Your set was amazing, with the chairs hanging in the air! I'll never forget it!" If you reach people the right way, they'll become ambassadors for your work, your theater company.

Those *Our Town* fans will tell their friends, children, and grand-children about it. Their excitement will be contagious. That's the kind of work I want to do.

During a run of *Children of a Lesser God* in Stockbridge, Mass-achusetts, in 2017, a woman came up to me after a show and said, "I have never seen a better twenty minutes in a play than what I saw tonight. I felt so human, so raw." That kind of feedback is powerful fuel. Joshua Jackson and Lauren Ridloff did amazing work in a play that most people think is about the struggles of being deaf. But it's really about our tendency to try to change people; our common refusal to see people for who they are in-stead of who we want them to be; and our unwillingness, or inability, to find the common ground we need when interacting with people who are fundamentally different than we are.

During the rehearsal of any show, I'll be sitting by myself, smil-ing and laughing.

Someone will say, "What are you thinking about?"

"I'm thinking about how I can get this to the next level. How I can make it better. I know I can be very critical of myself and my work, but I have to speak up when I don't like the way some-thing is playing. It might be good but I want it to be great. I was laughing at how I have never changed as a director. I just keep pushing."

Those thoughts run through my mind for every show. I'm con-stantly processing those ideas.

I ask myself questions all the time when I'm working on a show:

What would make a person who hates Kenny Leon come to see this show?

What would make a person who hates the theater come to see this show?

How can I get more people sitting in those seats to see what I am trying to do without me having to explain what I'm trying to do?

How can I get people to come to the theater and just enjoy the show?

How can I create a regular theatergoer?

With plays that I am directing, I have immediate and total control of the creative process. As the creative director of the True Colors Theatre Company in Atlanta, it's a little different. I run the theater but I'm away a lot. Still, I oversee all the productions. I come in during tech week and make sure all the plays maintain the level of quality we want for each show. I'm the boss but I don't want them to do what I would do. I just want them to be good. And I need to see it live onstage to know where each show stands.

I'm looking to see how the questions I ask myself have been answered by others.

In 2017, I hired a young guy who's done about three plays for us to direct a production of *Between Riverside and Crazy* by Stephen Adly Guirgis, which won the 2015 Pulitzer Prize for Drama. It's an intense play about life in New York involving police brutality, rent-controlled apartment living, and matters of life and death.

I came in to see where they were with the play. As I watched, I noticed that every scene with three characters or less was powerful. The scenes with seven or eight people onstage were a little confusing and I didn't know where to look. I remembered being a young director and struggling with how to handle a crowded stage.

I took the director aside and told him, "Look at all the scenes with more than three people."

"What do you mean?"

"You have them laid out in a linear way. You're losing control and focus. What you need to do is make it possible for people to watch what you want them to watch in one eye view. You don't want them looking all across the stage. If it's a scene with seven people, you move them in together. You sit somebody on the edge of the couch and have someone stand behind them. Have someone sit on the floor. You keep your focus tight. It's not a movie. You can't spread them out because they think they need more room and shoot it from three different angles."

He understood immediately.

I finished my thought by saying, "I'm going to give you something that I learned from August Wilson. Always be aware of who's witnessing the story. That will tell the audience where you want them to look."

Onstage in *Fences*, Troy and Rose are having a fight in the backyard. Gabe comes over and asks for a piece of watermelon. Rose tells him to go inside to the refrigerator and get it.

An inexperienced director would just have Gabe go into the house and disappear.

But a director who is paying attention would tell the actor playing Gabe, "Get the watermelon and come back to the screen door." That puts him right in the middle of the fight between Troy and Rose. He's eating the watermelon and watching them go at it. That makes the scene more interesting. The director is telling you where to look and he's telling you what he feels about it as well. Think of that when you have scenes with a lot of people.

It's such a joy to be able to pass that knowledge down. It

connects my experience to that young director and gives him a chance to grow and learn as well. And it helps me maintain the quality I want in the shows I am involved in presenting.

Being critical of myself and being careful about the projects I choose and the actors I cast have paid off. When I did *A Raisin in the Sun* in 2014, I was a better director than when I did it in 2004. I'm more skilled because I'm always trying to learn, whether it be from directing my own shows or reaching out to Lloyd Richards, Ruby Dee, and Ossie Davis for advice on *Raisin*. The main improvement I have made is that now I am paying attention to more things.

My directing is always affected by what is happening in the world or what is happening to me in my life. So, to try and revisit that play and make the 2014 production look like the 2004 production made no sense to me. It's ten years later. I am surely not the same man so my take on that play should not be the same.

I begin each production as if it's a new piece of theater with a new set of actors. I was working with ten different actors and I base a lot of my directing on what each individual actor's truth may be in delivering a character. By 2014, I was much more attuned to that part of it.

Earlier in my career, I would spend more time on the first act than I did on the second act. Now I know to spend equal time on every part of the play. The truth may manifest itself in different ways. If I never get to act two to explain and explore what act two is about, then I have shortchanged act two. You don't have to see everything you want in rehearsal. In the early days, I would work act one until I got what I wanted, likely at the expense of the rest of the show. Now I know to just go over it a couple of times and move on. Let the actors find it over time. For the whole play.

I approach many aspects of directing differently now than when I started out. For my early directing efforts, I focused on the text. I prepare differently today. I read different things in my preparation to expand what I bring to the production's look and feel. If I'm doing a play that takes place in 1959, I'll read up on that era.

For Lorraine Hansberry and *Raisin*, I read a lot of James Baldwin because they were friends. I read a lot of his stuff and saw how it informed the play.

In 2014, I was more interested in Lorraine herself because I found out that many people had not even heard her voice before. But I had heard her 1959 interview with Studs Terkel and found it captivating. I mentioned it to my producer, Scott Rudin. He said, "Kenny, you could play that interview at the beginning of the show as people are walking into the theater."

With that encouragement, we arranged for it to happen that way. Not turned up loud but at a level you could hear but would have to strive to catch it. In the background if you wanted it that way but audible if you were inclined to listen.

In the interview, Lorraine talks about capturing the specific to portray the universal, how commercial Broadway was and about how we should have more theater in education around the country. What I wanted was for people to hear the strength and power and conviction in her voice. That became important to me.

In 2004, I was not thinking about that. My attitude was, "Let's get this play up and going." I thought I knew what the play was about. "Let's make it funny when it's appropriate, and let's make it somber in the more serious sections." But over time, I've come to understand the craft better. Each play and its presentation depend on the cast you have.

Comparing how I approached those two productions, ten years apart, is why I feel confident that my best work is ahead of me. I'm evolving.

I'm learning how to deal with people better. I'm good at blending inexperienced actors with stage veterans. I'm learning how to get the most out of my actors.

I'm better at lighting. For *Children*, we dealt carefully with the color palette for various reasons. We can't put Lauren Ridloff in that particular yellow dress because it's going to fight the lights or fight the other colors. And if it's too yellow, she'll look like she has no clothes on. And we have a black actor and a white actor. The light looks different on the black actor so I have to look through each scene. Is Lauren being lit equally to Joshua Jackson? If we make this change for him, what does it do to her? These concerns come to me naturally now, and I have a much better sense of what to do than I did years ago.

I'm better at sculpting the picture and integrating sound and controlling focus.

These improvements in my craft are to be expected, after all. In any field, you ought to be improving all the time. These are my tools, and I have to take care of them if I want to keep answering the most important questions in the affirmative.

Is this project going to reach more people than my last one?
Am I getting better?

Make Your Place in the World

My grandmother Mamie and my mother showed me a way to live. Their lives have been examples of all I want to be.

The father figures in my life have had the opposite effect. My father, Leroy, was a disinterested parent who was never more than on the fringe of my life. My stepfather, Johnnie, was a good man who raised three kids who were not his own. I respect him for that. But in most other ways, I didn't like how he met the world and the way he dealt with young folks. Neither one of them represented what I wanted to be as a man or a father.

Just as I am glad to have had those two women in my life, I am also glad to have had those two men. By watching them and interacting with them, I learned what I did not want to be. I dealt with my life so as not to turn out like they did. It's not an accident that I never called either one of them Daddy.

I don't live with Leroy's remoteness from his children and the attending responsibilities. And luckily, I have not had his problems with substance abuse. I didn't want to abuse anything after seeing Leroy contend with "fillin' my little pocket" every day.

Unlike Johnnie, I want to have a loving relationship with young people. I have been caring and supportive of Maria, my stepdaughter. I would move heaven and earth for my grandson, Gabriel. And in my work with younger people, I have been a devoted father figure to many actors such as P. Diddy, Ariana Grande, Lauren Ridloff, and all of my August Wilson kids.

I have consciously tried to fill my life and my actions with gentleness, the lack of which defined Johnnie for me.

Johnnie started from a position of distrust in other people. He just assumed everyone was trying to pull one over on him or was lying to him to be in his world. He approached the world harshly with a head-on roughness that was bruising to those around him. Get them before they get you. Maybe he felt that was his only option. But all I learned from his way was to find another way.

Johnnie liked fishing but I didn't see him take a particular interest in nature. His worldview did not include much that was gentle, soft, or warm. He did not take the time to see the beauty all around us. He never saw anything romantic or sentimental in the way a family can be together. He didn't believe in the future of his children and that they could build on and improve what his generation had.

Johnnie and Leroy both looked at life as a time and place to stand where you are. If you can just stand up for yourself, that's enough.

When I came along, it was about more than standing up.

Let me stand up for everyone. Let me lead another generation somewhere we haven't been.

My insistent reach for what is possible, yet not obvious, was

greater than their ability to comprehend it. They did not understand my approach to the world, and they saw no reason to
believe the world could be different from what they knew.

I acknowledge the practical aspects of their attitudes.

Hey, Kenny! Get out there and rake the yard!

But I believe Leroy and Johnnie, one absent and the other very
distrustful, held me back from being the most I could be. They
may have understood the world as it was, but the women in my
life had a strong feeling about what the world could be.

Leroy and Johnnie sought to survive. I sought to thrive.

The sacrifices that Mamie and Mom made were in service to
something they believed in without seeing. My grandmother was
well into her seventies before she saw a live theater production,
my chosen field. Her reaction was:

*Of course! Kenny has made his world what he wanted it to be.
That's what I expected. He did things that no one in our family had
done before.*

My mother has had the same reaction to the things my work
has revealed to her about the world. And her response has always
been a joyous and happy one because I found my own path and a
way to be happy and a way to make a difference. They'd both have
been just as happy if I'd found the same fulfillment as a lawyer or
a teacher. Or an astronaut.

They wanted to give me the courage and self-confidence to go
out in the world and find my life with honor and dignity. They
wanted me to know that I could define my time on earth as I
wanted, that I could aim as high, far, and wide as I wanted. And
that I would hit the mark.

Leroy and Johnnie said, "Take your place in the world."

Grandma and Mom said, "Make your place in the world."

I still try to live a life that is worthy of my grandmother's memory. That keeps me going.

Thinking of her, and the women in my family before her, has been my lifelong inspiration. I don't mean to knock the men, really I don't, but those women had a way of believing in you and encouraging you to go for...whatever you decide is a better life. They could not see that better life. Or name it. But they believed, they *knew*, it was there. The men in my life that raised me simply could not summon that faith in me or my future.

There have been some men along the way that pushed me in the right direction, who tried to help me look beyond my immediate surroundings. Mr. Pope taught me how to play the violin when I was in junior high school.

"Come, on, Leon. Pick up that violin. Practice. Work at it. Get better. You could have a career playing the violin."

I didn't believe him at the time and never took it as seriously as I should have. Mr. Pope was a bit ahead of his time, going out of his way to nurture me in a nontraditional manner. Safe to say he was the only man telling me to think about being a musician for a living. But maybe his approach nudged me in the direction of the arts. I kept my violin for a long time. I used to play it late at night to relax. I think I lost it in the divorce, but I plan to get another one soon.

Sam Jackson and I are friends but he's a bit older and has been a true mentor to me. He and his wife, LaTanya Richardson, were the first people I ever saw on a live stage, back when I was in college. My only thought was:

Shit! That guy's having fun!

He has counseled me in many ways for about forty years. He always used to tell me, "I'm from the South, where grown folks get up and go to work." I have always remembered Sam's approach and work ethic. He'd always say to me, "Hey, Leon, you got that job?" Because our work is project work. When one ends, another one better begin. We're always reinforcing that with each other.

We got to get up and work. We don't have time to fool around. After you turn eighteen, you're out in the world. Taking care of business.

Even today, after I've built a good career and found success, Sam will be there to bolster me. In the summer of 2017, the Emmy nominations came out and *Hairspray Live!* was eligible. Sam called me and said, "Well, I guess that TV musical directed itself. Y'all got seven nominations but the director didn't get one. How does that happen?" I don't worry about awards but it's nice to get that nod from an old friend. (Phylicia Rashad had the same comment about the 2004 *Raisin in the Sun* and the Tonys. Good friends always show up with kind words to let you know you're in their thoughts.)

Another mentor of mine, Dr. Joseph Lowery, echoed Sam's attitude. Dr. Lowery told me that his father never saw their house in the daytime. He left before dawn and came back after dusk. Work and dedication are part of a successful life. Sam and Dr. Lowery both told me and showed me that truth.

My mother's oldest brother, and Mamie's oldest child, is my uncle Lucian, still going strong today at ninety-six. He owned a very successful cattle ranch and farm. He and his family didn't live as far out in the country as Grandma, and they had a brick ranch house with many rooms and a two-car garage. I knew him first when I was very young, but I always knew him as a strong, powerful, successful black man. He showed me what was possible at a young age and was a positive, familiar role model for me.

I've been lucky to have these and other black men to show me the way, to hold me to standards, and to build me up. And I must say that Leroy and Johnnie taught me things that have proved useful my whole life. Johnnie taught me how to fish and he introduced me to the fun and camaraderie of watching sports on TV. He also helped my mother persuade me to keep going to church. And Leroy definitely showed me the beauty in just being able to laugh at life and not take anything too seriously. I've used that skill more than once.

But the main source of my energy and drive is the power of my mom and my grandmother both saying to me, "You can create a world that's different. I don't know what you're gonna do, but you can do that."

Their support of me was and is very spiritual. They see it as a continuum. I know for a fact that I am the heir of August Wilson, Lorraine Hansberry, and Lloyd Richards. And all of my African American forebears across all professions and disciplines. Part of what I am doing as an artist and as a person on this planet is making things right for all of us across time. We won't know until we die what it all means and how different times and worlds overlap. I believe they're all connected. And I know that Grandma Mamie would take joy in where I am today and what I am able to do creatively. She helped to bring it about, after all.

Every day, I thank the Lord for my grandmother and my mother. The force of their belief in me is why I keep pushing forward. I try to honor them and have always wanted them to take joy in what I have been able to accomplish. Because the world did not allow it in their lives. But they prayed me into a world where anything was possible.

They believed in my future before I was born.

God Don't Care What You Wear

I wear sneakers all the time. Tennis shoes or whatever you want to call them. Taking an afternoon walk in Atlanta or attending a premiere on Broadway. It's a signature style statement, I guess, but there's some substance there, too.

Many years ago, a dear friend of mine was quite ill. He had AIDS but we didn't know it at the time. We just knew he was very sick; in fact, he was dying.

Back then, I wore red Reeboks a lot, nearly every day. I was visiting my friend and he looked at my shoes and laughed a little. He said, "Man, don't ever change. Always wear those red Reeboks!"

It wasn't exactly his dying request, but when he did pass, I remembered his advice and decided that I would keep on wearing those red Reeboks in his honor. He knew me well and I was touched that he'd told me not to change.

A little while later, I was talking to my grandmother about wearing tennis shoes with suits and maybe even in church. She said, "Well, honey, take you wherever you go. Be yourself. But I don't think you can just wear red. You should wear different colors and you should accessorize. If you're wearing red sneakers, maybe you put on a little red bow tie. God don't care what you wear but just look nice. Have some class."

She always said that to me.

"Grandma, I'm going to New York for the first time. I'm going to see a Broadway show. I don't know what to wear."

"Now, baby, just take you wherever you go," she'd say. "Don't worry about anybody else. Just take you."

Not long after that red sneaker conversation, she passed away. In my mourning and coming to terms with her loss, I decided that one way I would keep her near me would be to continue wearing sneakers every day and to accessorize as she suggested. I'd mix and match shirts, jackets, sneakers, and pocket squares to have that class Grandma Mamie recommended.

By then, I was known a bit in Atlanta and my sneakers were part of my story. Somebody wrote to a newspaper in Atlanta that somebody should "give Kenny a sneaker deal."

Soon after, Reebok came through and offered to have a discussion about me and my sneakers. I wanted them to give $200,000 for the Children's Theatre at the Alliance, where I worked.

They declined that idea but said they would clothe me with Reebok stuff and revisit the donation later. As it turned out, they never came through with the money for the children's theater so I called off that arrangement.

Then I started to wear Nikes at my own cost.

A few years back, Sam Jackson introduced me to the folks at Adidas. He said to them, "Look, Kenny is a famous director and he's on a lot of red carpets. He already wears sneakers all the time.

Why shouldn't they be Adidas?" I came to an agreement with Adidas.

While there is no formal financial stipulation, Adidas does a lot for me and the causes I support. They have supported my True Colors Theatre and they have supplied golf shoes to participants in my golf gala and fund-raiser. Sometimes as many as 159 pairs. They have also provided me with jackets, bags, and backpacks emblazoned with the True Colors logo.

So, yes, after a long history of staying dedicated to the memory of my friend and my grandmother, I have a sneaker deal, just like LeBron James and Stephen Curry. Maybe not exactly like theirs but a deal is a deal. It is one of the perks of my line of work and I don't take it for granted. I get to dress the way I want and honor loved ones. But there's more to it.

Whenever I do workshops at schools, young kids want to talk about my sneakers. I tell them, "Remember that your tennis shoes can be a conversation starter. When you meet some new kids, you can say, 'What are you wearing? Oh, I got the new so-and-so's.' It can help break the ice, and soon you'll be comfortable enough to talk about anything going on in your lives."

Wearing sneakers every day also reminds me to stay grounded and to remember that I'm just a country boy from Tallahassee, Florida. I look down at them twenty or thirty times a day. And when I do, I then look up and smile at my grandmother. Because of my tennis shoes, she's never far from my mind. So, while I may have a sneaker deal, I'd wear them every day even if I didn't.

I'd never miss those chances to connect with Grandma Mamie.

The Wisdom of My Elders

In 2013, plans were under way for me to direct a Broadway revival of *A Raisin in the Sun*. We were going to do it in the same theater where *Raisin* debuted, the Barrymore Theatre on West Forty-Seventh Street. As we began work, I was excited and proud.

This production would be my third time working on this American classic. In 2004, I directed a Broadway production of *Raisin*. And in 2008, I directed a movie version for ABC.

Raisin is a very spiritual play with a lot of richness and depth. And I feel very strongly about supporting the work of an African American woman. There was talk that by 2014 the play had become a bit dated. I could not disagree more. I feel it is one of the top five best American plays and the others, such as *A Streetcar Named Desire*, *Death of a Salesman*, or *Long Day's Journey into Night*, are revisited every four or five years. Why not the same treatment for *A Raisin in the Sun*? I had not one misgiving about directing this play on Broadway ten years after my last effort. None at all.

214

Raisin is a play that keeps on giving. Lorraine's piercing and majestic writing about family, love, truth, and the pursuit of your dreams, no matter the obstacles, will always be relevant. It's set in 1959 on the South Side of Chicago, but it can be today or tomorrow and anyplace in the world. The issues and struggles Lorraine wrote about are essentially human and will always be there for people to face and figure out.

I was excited about the ensemble we had gathered and had plans to make an intimate production of a big play.

As I have mentioned, one of my favorite things to do, and something I consider to be essential, is to sit and talk and drink in the wisdom of my elders. My way of honoring my elders is to include them in my work and life, to have them join me. Nothing makes me happier than to be able to talk to an older person and hear his or her story. Doing this generational exchange is purely enjoyable in every case. But when I talk to veteran actors, directors, and producers, I'm not only having a good time, but getting better at my job. You can't leave a conversation with an experienced old pro without learning something. And I have no plans to stop learning.

Without a doubt, this penchant I have is yet another gift from Grandma Mamie. Her ease with me during my childhood is what allows me, draws me, to sit and talk to older folks. I have always known it to be a loving, worthwhile, and important thing to do.

When David Binder hired me to direct the 2004 production of *Raisin*, I went to Lloyd Richards's home in New York City. Lloyd directed the Broadway premiere of *Raisin* in 1959 and had gone on to an accomplished career in the theater, working closely with August Wilson. Lloyd directed the first August Wilson play on

Broadway, *Ma Rainey's Black Bottom*, in 1984 and won a Tony for his direction of the premiere of *Fences* in 1987. He was the dean of the Yale School of Drama, and he nurtured the work of many young, aspiring playwrights such as Christopher Durang, David Henry Hwang, and Wendy Wasserstein. Lloyd was a tremendous director and a man of the theater with an impressive legacy.

Our paths had crossed a few times, and he knew I was a huge fan of his work. After all, his production of *Fences* forever enhanced my relationship to the theater. I visited Lloyd to let him know that I'd been offered the play. My plan was to share some thoughts. I wanted him to hear from me that we had no plans to diminish or obscure in any way what he had done with *Raisin*. If anything, one of our goals was to honor his achievement. I wanted to build on it by bringing some new eyes to it.

We sat in his apartment for a few hours and talked about the play. We had a great exchange of thoughts and ideas, and I was very glad I'd made the effort to meet with him. I could not tell you exactly how or where that conversation affected my direction of the play, but I do know that I took in all Lloyd had to say and his inspiration infused my thinking and directing.

I invited Lloyd to be my guest at the opening of *Raisin in the Sun* on April 26, 2004. On the day of the show, Lloyd sent flowers to the green room for me. I knew what it meant—that he could not be there himself. *Raisin* was a big part of who Lloyd had become as a person and a director. His career was just beginning in 1959, and being there for that opening night in 2004 would somehow take away from his memories of what he had done all those years earlier. It was beautiful and touching to me because I got it. I sent him a note to let him know that I understood and that those flowers meant a lot to me, as did the conversation we'd had all those months earlier. He was certainly there in spirit.

Shortly after my visit with Lloyd, I met with Ruby Dee and Ossie Davis. Both Ruby and Ossie are closely associated with *Raisin*. Ruby had played Walter's wife, Ruth, in the original Broadway production, though she auditioned for the role of the younger Beneatha. Ossie took over the role of Walter during its initial run on Broadway when Sidney Poitier left the show. Ruby was also in the well-received 1961 *Raisin* movie that featured the original Broadway cast. I knew their familiarity with the play and its themes could help this new production.

I told them what I'd told Lloyd, that I felt we were all involved in a long process of passing things down from generation to generation. I wanted their insights, and a few weeks before we opened, I invited Ossie and Ruby to come by some preview rehearsals to give me notes. At first, I didn't expect them to come by, but Ruby was at those preview rehearsals as much as anybody. And they did what I asked—watched rehearsals and gave me comments on what they saw. I noticed a lot of Ruby's comments were about Beneatha even though she played Ruth. She respected that character and was drawn to Beneatha's complexity. It also told me that Ruby understood her like no other character onstage. She had a depth of understanding about how that woman should behave, about her choices, and how she lived in and moved through the world. Beneatha was always ahead of herself. She was always politically, socially, sexually...in every way she was ahead of anybody around her.

I have always thought of that role as being Lorraine Hansberry herself. She died at thirty-four, but she gave the world so much in those short years.

Ruby loved that whole play and you could feel it when she talked about it.

It meant a lot to me to include Lloyd, Ruby, and Ossie in my new production of *Raisin*. They had worked so hard to get that play to Broadway in 1959. A black drama by a black woman on Broadway in 1959? That was a tall order and they made history. It was so great to get their feedback and their blessing.

My plan, of course, was to do something different because we were in different times. I have fond memories of that production, too, because Phylicia Rashad was the first African American woman to win the Tony for best leading actress in a play. It's a sobering thought when you start to think about all the black women who had graced the stage before her. Still, it was fitting that the performance of a character written by Lorraine Hansberry would accomplish that milestone.

Later on, when I got the chance to direct a filmed version of the play, I remembered that Lloyd didn't get the same chance. That's the way it was back in 1961—a black man was not going to get to direct a movie, even if he had already directed the play on Broadway. In a way he did, though, because they basically shot his production for the movie. Sidney and Ruby were in the earlier movie, and my cast for the play made the movie. I felt I was doing it for Lloyd as much as myself.

Before rehearsals for *Raisin* in 2014 began, I was in Los Angeles and Denzel Washington, whom I cast in *Raisin*, asked me to meet him for lunch. When the meal was over, he asked me to jump in his car. We were going to meet someone special.

Less than an hour later, I was sitting in Sidney Poitier's living room.

In 1967, Poitier was in three movies (three!) that represent what I would like to do in every project I undertake. *In the Heat of the Night*, *To Sir, with Love*, and *Guess Who's Coming to Dinner* have many things in common, but the most important are that they deal with questions of race, they are entertaining, and they were, quite simply, hits. They were successful in the ways that all theater and movies projects need to be, if you want to stay in the game while retaining your pride and honor.

In America, we often talk of how an athlete "had a great year." Winning a championship and the Most Valuable Player Award, leading the league in key stats, or setting important records.

In 1967, Sidney Poitier had a really great year. Definitely my MVP. And inspiration to this day.

And in 1959, he originated the role of Walter Lee Younger in *A Raisin in the Sun*, the role in which I was about to direct Denzel.

That wonderful afternoon, we had a great conversation with Sidney about many topics. And we discussed *Raisin* and he generously shared his insights and memories with us. He couldn't have been more gracious and encouraging. At the end of the conversation, Denzel and I asked him about one lingering issue that was slightly bothering us.

There were people who were saying that Denzel was too old for the part.

"Mr. Poitier, what do we do about those people?" we said.

"Fuck them!"

Sometimes advice from older people unravels slowly, revealing itself over time through many stories and conversations.

And other times, it falls onto you with a quick and breathtaking clarity.

We never thought about Denzel's age again.

Afro-centric Stories on
Euro-centric Stages

As I look forward in my working life, I am blessed to have options. My network is wide, and I know a lot of people who look for projects in the same way that I do, with an eye toward *challenging* the audience, *entertaining* the audience, and most important, *reaching* a wide audience. I ask myself many questions when considering whether or not to do something. At this point in my life, a very important part of my decision process is assessing whether this project or that project will help me reach people who might not have seen many of my previous plays, movies, or television work. I do see a bit of the preacher in my goals and visions and in how I have conducted my career. I want to spread the word about inclusion and reaching out to others. I want to talk about how we can help one another if we take the time to see and understand each other. And I want to do that in a way that is entertaining for the public and profitable for the people who have invested in my work and given me the chance to live out my professional dreams.

As always, I try to stay true to myself and have the courage to declare what it is I want to do and what I do not want to do. The process is never easy, but it is something that I am getting better at and something that I will always hold to the highest standards. Frankly, I'm hard on myself because I judge myself in ways that are very serious and important to me personally. Success, to me, is not measured in only one way.

I'll never forget a piece of advice that I received from two men I greatly admire for their achievements and their unwavering dedication to the discussion of race in America.

The abbreviated run of *Holler if Ya Hear Me* on Broadway in 2014 was a big disappointment to me. Even though we all knew that the subject matter, the daily struggles of people living in poor, inner-city communities in America, would be challenging for ticket sales, we hoped that we could stay around long enough for word of mouth to take over. I also wanted to honor the memory and salute the poetry of Tupac Shakur. But the show didn't find an audience in time, and it closed after seven weeks. We missed the mark and I felt bad about it. I felt bad for my friend Todd Kreidler, who wrote the book for the show, and for everyone involved. It was a true passion project and I was wounded by its demise. Broadway productions are a business and I know that the show didn't close due to a personal failing of mine. Or anyone else's. But I really wanted that work to have a longer life because I believed in it and felt it was an important story to tell.

One evening shortly after the show had closed, I was walking in New York and a taxi pulled over near me. From the cab emerged two of my heroes: Harry Belafonte and Dr. Cornel West.

In his work as an actor, singer, songwriter, and political activist,

Belafonte has done what I have tried to do. He, like August Wilson, is a committed artist.

West is a leading voice in America on race and class.

Both Harry and Cornel have supported my work, have provided encouragement, and have let me know they see and value the importance of what I try to do. Cornel is about my age but Harry is thirty years older. His thoughts and feelings are particularly important to me. He has seen it all in America, and few know the complexity of the African American experience better than Harry Belafonte. And few entertainers have so consistently addressed African American issues in their work.

As they stepped from their cab, they greeted me.

"Brother Leon!" said Cornel. "How nice to see you!"

We hugged and began talking. We got around to discussing *Holler if Ya Hear Me.* Harry mentioned that he had seen and really enjoyed the show. And I expressed my disappointment in the brevity of the show's run, frustration and regret evident in my voice and on my face.

"You're looking at it the wrong way," said Cornel gently.

"He's right, Kenny," said Harry. "What you did was admirable and strong. You told an Afro-centric story on a Euro-centric stage. That's very hard to do."

"The length of the run is not important," said Cornel. "What matters is that your show made it to Broadway. And a lot of people saw it. You probably changed or opened a few minds along the way. And you made it a little easier for anyone who tries to do something similar in the future. We keep an eye on all of your projects and we love to see what you are doing. Keep moving forward, Brother Leon."

I am not wired to see any nobility in my work. I'm a country boy from Tallahassee, Florida, and always will be. Due to the grace of God, I was raised by two amazing women and I live in the aftermath of their love, care, and wisdom. Cornel West, Harry Belafonte, and the generations of extraordinary people before them taught me so many things that I have boiled down to the title of this book: *Take You Wherever You Go*. Believe me when I tell you that I do not look at things in a way that is more complicated than that thought. Be true to yourself and things will work out and you will achieve more that way than what any kind of compromise might bring. And if you make a break from your true self, you may succeed but it will not be a peaceful success because you'll know of the betrayal better than anyone. This principle that I have made the center of my life is both simple and hard. I'll be working on it for all of my days. It will always be my measure.

I have trouble seeing anything grand in my work or my life because that perspective would not help me. I have, and only want, the perspective of a country boy from Tallahassee. That young boy now directs plays on Broadway and on NBC Television. I get that. But I do not want to lose the driving, animating idea that got me where I am.

Brother Belafonte and Brother West probably know that. So they, as the cultural leaders they are, knew instinctively in that sudden, unexpected moment to say what they said to me. They told me something that I needed to hear but probably could not tell myself. They were being truthful and would not have said it if they didn't feel it. That alone was powerful to me.

But that night, on the streets of New York, I was being honest in my assessment of the Broadway production of *Holler if Ya Hear Me.* I was disappointed that the show did not have a longer run and, therefore, reach more people. And I was disappointed for the producers that we weren't more successful with that show. I couldn't be breezy about it and say, "Well, we tried our best and it didn't work out." I had made it with my heart, and I took the results to heart.

But I needed to hear that the effort itself made it worthwhile. I needed to hear that it was, yes, grand and noble of us to try to tell the story of life in America's inner cities using the brilliant poetry of that black American man and artist, one so misunderstood in his all-too-brief time with us.

We had honored Tupac Shakur with that show. The length of the run, while important, was not the right measuring stick and certainly not the only one. I was too close to it to see that.

That one brief conversation with Harry and Cornel was significant for me. It set me straight with its wisdom, care, and love. It reminded me that my values and goals were still very much intact and still very much worth protecting. At certain times in your life, that kind of message has to be delivered to you by others, generous souls offering support and encouragement.

They were there for me that day, and I will always try to be there for others whenever I get the chance.

I revived *Holler if Ya Hear Me* in September 2017 in Atlanta with my True Colors Theatre Company and in partnership with some of the historically black colleges and universities in Atlanta—Spelman College, Morehouse College, and Clark Atlanta. The hope is that the show will catch fire and places like Detroit, Baltimore, Tampa, and

Birmingham will clamor for a production to come to their theaters. If that happens, as Todd Kreidler says, then this show will have had Broadway as its tryout and the rest of the country as its triumph.

Because of Harry and Cornel, I was able to return to that show with energy and pride in the knowledge that simply undertaking that work, that story, was an honorable effort and a success all its own. After the first week of the *Holler* revival, I spoke to the minister of my church. He saw the play and wants to do a community event after the show one night that centers around what is happening in our inner cities. We are losing our fourteen- and fifteen-year-old kids. And that's what the play is about: *saving* our young teenagers.

* * *

My chance meeting with Harry and Cornel took me back to the porch with my grandma. And to those long talks I had with August Wilson and Todd Kreidler during August's last weeks. It also reminded me of that first time I heard *Fences* on Broadway and felt the importance of African American culture.

I've learned so much from my grandmother, my mother, and August that I find myself looking for ways to stay connected to them, to find voices similar to theirs among these mentors, colleagues, and contemporaries in my life.

I will always draw on the wisdom of these voices when I choose my projects and what stories to tell.

Because no matter what, I will always be a country boy, Annie Ruth's son, and Mamie's grandson.

Acknowledgments

To Jennifer Thompson with love; you have always been my rock and foundation.

I owe a great debt to the generation of men and women before me who understood that vision and courage are important to assure a more beautiful American future. I salute Maynard Jackson, Ruby Dee, Jennings Hertz, Max Shaffer, Ossie Davis, Harry Belafonte, Joseph Lowery, Frank Wittow, Lloyd Richards, Ms. Howard (my eighth-grade history teacher), and Mr. Lawrence Pope (my seventh-grade violin teacher).

Diahann Carroll has always inspired me, and I treasure the writings of Lorraine Hansberry and Zora Neale Hurston.

Thanks to Gretchen Young at Grand Central for the countless hours of support, editing, hand holding, passion, and love. This book would not exist without her devotion to it. And thanks as well to her wonderful assistant, Katherine Stopa.

There are no better agents than Cait Hoyt and Joe Machota from CAA.

John Hassan, you are indeed my brother—we take this walk together.

Thank you to True Colors Theatre Company for lending me to the world.

The Wilson and Leon Families of Tallahassee, Florida—I have only love for you all.

Samuel L. Jackson, that older brother I never had. And to his wife, LaTanya, and daughter, Zoe—thanks for the love.

Janece Shaffer, for getting this whole thing started, and David Davidson, for encouraging me to keep telling stories.

Denzel Washington—always there!

Phylicia Rashad, forever my artistic soul mate. And thanks to Condola Rashad for letting me teach her.

Stan Lathan, who listened when no one else in the business in LA would talk to me.

Todd Kreidler, my encouraging brother forever.

Constanza Romero, for her vision and nurturing of the August Wilson Estate.

Jennifer McEwen, Marion Young, and all of the partners of the National August Wilson Monologue Competition.

Neil Meron and Craig Zadan, for always believing in the talent.

I have learned so much from Bob Greenblatt, an executive with passion and vision.

Chris Manos, my theater godfather, who has always inspired and encouraged a life in the theater.

Timothy Near, because she was the person who encouraged me to grow.

My early agents, Joyce Ketay and Susan Weaving.

My first manager, Johnnie Planco, who always believed.

Riley Temple, Barbara Lebow, and the theater teachers Joan Lewis and Michele Rubin, who got me going in college.

The example of Dr. Julius Erving.

The endless hours of help from my tireless assistant, Jacob Demlow.

And to the memory of my dear friend and great actor Bill Nunn.